BOOKS BY MARVIN BELL

POETRY

New and Selected Poems   1987

Drawn by Stones, by Earth, by Things that Have Been in the Fire   1984

These Green-Going-to-Yellow   1981

Stars Which See, Stars Which Do Not See   1977

Residue of Song   1974

The Escape into You   1971

A Probable Volume of Dreams   1969

LIMITED EDITIONS

Woo Havoc (pamphlet)   1971

Things We Dreamt We Died For   1966

Poems for Nathan and Saul (pamphlet)   1966

POETRY COLLABORATIONS

Segues: A Correspondence in Poetry (with William Stafford)   1983

PROSE

Old Snow Just Melting: Essays and Interviews   1983

NEW AND
SELECTED
POEMS

MARVIN BELL
NEW AND
SELECTED
POEMS

New York ATHENEUM 1987

New poems in this collection first appeared in THE AMERICAN POETRY REVIEW (*Long Island*); THE BREAD LOAF ANTHOLOGY OF CONTEMPORARY AMERICAN POETRY (*Song for a Little Bit of Breath*); THE GEORGIA REVIEW (*Replica*); THE IOWA REVIEW (CLASSIFIED and *Where He Stood: A Photographer's Portfolio*); NEW AMERICAN REVIEW (*Study Guide for the* Odyssey); THE NEW YORKER (*Wednesday*); PLAINSONG (*Music Lessons, She Can't Stop Herself* and *Trees Standing Bare*); QUARTERLY WEST (*In My Nature: 3 Corrective Dialogues, The Pill* and *The Politics of an Object*); and THE SEATTLE REVIEW (*Six Poems to Tao Yuan-ming*).

TO HARRY FORD

CONTENTS

Contents

from Residue of Song (1974)

Previously Uncollected

from Stars Which See, Stars Which Do Not See (1977)

Contents

from These Green-Going-to-Yellow (1981)

from Drawn by Stones, by Earth, by Things that Have Been in the Fire (1984)

New Poems

FROM

Things We Dreamt
We Died For

(1 9 6 6)

The Admission

If you love me,
say so.
Snow piles; bridges burn
behind me; I
imagine
that I am alone
and have not
turned toward you so
before. I forget
openings I had not thought of
turning toward,
to tell you, and to tell you
to tell me.
The surroundings affect us;
it is a cause
for love
that you call it
something logical,
taking pleasure in
our finding
ourselves here.
Tell me landscapes
are frames of mind.
I believe words have meaning.
No gift will do.
Tell me what it means
to you.

Treetops

My father moves through the South hunting duck.
It is warm, he has appeared
like a ship, surfacing, where he floats, face up,
through the ducklands. Over the tops
of trees duck will come, and he strains
not to miss seeing the first of each flock,
although it will be impossible to shoot one
from such an angle, face up like that
in a floating coffin where the lid obstructs
half a whole view, if he has a gun.
Afterlives are full of such hardships.

One meets, for example, in one's sinlessness,
high water and our faithlessness,
so the dead wonder if they are imagined
but they are not quite.

How could they know we know
when the earth shifts deceptively
to set forth ancestors to such pursuits?
My father will be asking, Is this fitting?
And I think so—I, who, with the others,
coming on the afterlife after the fact
in a dream, in a probable volume, in a
probable volume of dreams, think so.

What Songs the Soldiers Sang

Those with few images, lyrics
in which doing and undoing
prevailed, there were conclusions
and many epithets.
To hell with what it might look like!
The idea of breakfast, to take one
example, was a favorite
in the evenings. Also,
the way fields shut down,
and the weight of the equipment.
In choruses full of objects
nothing civilian moved
but loud young men bent on silence
and backbreaking labors.
It was natural to welcome them
with triumphal marches.
Many would return in halves.
The songs, too, about their singing, are lies.
The truth is that some songs were obscene
and that there were no words for others.

A History of Cameras and Cameramen

Once it took 5 minutes and 20 seconds to make a portrait. ("Dark
   colored walls and hangings and only one window . . . Cloudy
   dull") That, from *Interesting Pointers for Kodakers,* 1903.
Every expansion of the chest, every crumbling exhalation, every blink
   bent its reflections into the pebbled black box to blend the already
   hazy film with some of the atmosphere pushed against it.
Association. The result was soft—sepia and cream—5 minutes and 20
   seconds of the subject, 5′ 20″ of fine-grain absorption.
It is why no one is seen running in Brady's civil war. It is why the
   backgrounds and corners of Gardner's photos of the war, circa
   1861, leave us no focus but the heaving breasts of the medalled
   living, the composed breasts of the dead. It is why the shutters of
   their boxes of light opened and closed like a period, the shutters
   able to capture nothing in between
Life and death. In short, they were limited to extensive exposure.

We are not. I can squeeze the lights and darks of you through a pinhole
   so perfect onto a film plane so focused upon by a fine lens that one
   one-thousandth of a second is enough to engrave a topographic
   image of you, enough to frame you in a background so textured
   with simultaneous detail that we know from the processed film
It can never happen again. Bellows, tilts, swings, attachments—all are
   refinements for measuring and dividing the infinite combinations
   of foot-candles which exist in the real world, in the real black
   and optic world.
Let the Bradys and Gardners, the drunken artists who shake their
   cameras, who would return to the spongy exposures of absorption
   in the frail manner of the old hooded and bulb-squeezing
   formalists to whom states of pure existence or absence only were
   compositional, watch out. We are here more perfectly, as in all
   things, with quick new eyes and cameras, with what nimble
   machines!; automatically, we are
Beyond life and death.
And what they did well we have left behind.

The Israeli Navy

The Israeli Navy,
sailing to the end of the world,
stocked with grain
and books black with God's verse,
turned back,
rather than sail on the Sabbath.
Six days, was the consensus,
was enough for anyone.

So the world, it was concluded,
was three days wide
in each direction,
allowing three days back.
And Saturdays were given over
to keeping close,
while Sundays the Navy,
all decked out in white
and many-colored skull caps,
would sail furiously,
trying to go off the deep end.

Yo-ho-ho, would say the sailors,
for six days.
While on the shore their women moaned.

For years, their boats were slow,
and all show.
And they turned into families
on the only land they knew.

Fairy Tales

When he finds in myth
his reality,
once is enough. No dissent
is possible, no other
possibility exists
than that in the books
with no faces, than that
faced in the books
by characters uncharacteristic
in their fair and sufficient
abilities, and in their useful
and beautiful faces—
such blanks as are filled in
by him who needs to, or who
naturally would.
One right ending—
the hero in his garden,
incomparably green;
the best of possibilities—
makes up for more likely
endings than are, after all,
wished possible. Overboard
is the place to go to
when too much is imaginable,
for there there is nothing
less imaginable
than too much of anything.
In life it is sufficient
to have everything.
There enough is enough.

Things We Dreamt We Died For

Flags of all sorts.
The literary life.
Each time we dreamt we'd done
the gentlemanly thing,
covering our causes
in closets full of bones
to remove ourselves forever
from dearest possibilities,
the old weapons re-injured us,
the old armies conscripted us,
and we gave in to getting even,
a little less like us
if a lot less like others.
Many, thus, gained fame
in the way of great plunderers,
retiring to the university
to cultivate grand plunder-gardens
in the service of literature,
the young and no more wars.
Their continuing tributes
make them our greatest saviours,
whose many fortunes are followed
by the many who have not one.

The Condition

The darkness within me is growing.
I am turned out.

Thought feeds on it
even as the body is eaten.

Its goodness is without a face.
But it convinces me to look.

It can fade from now until doomsday.
It will not fade.

In the night I see it shining,
like a thing seen.

My Hate

My hate is like ripe fruit
from an orchard, which is mine.

I sink my teeth into it.
I nurse on its odd shapes.

I have grafted every new variety,
walked in my bare feet,

rotting and detached,
on the fallen ones.

Vicious circle. Unfriendly act.
I am eating the whole world.

In the caves of my ill will
I must be stopped.

Changes

I have hung and hung around.
When I say so, nothing changes.

Do cranes tip over?
Cranes tip over.
Also, houses burn.

In the forest I come to a clearing.
In the rain the trees overcome me.

I am liked. I give in.
I am swallowed in wood.

Upright birds. A sense of well-being.
At last I look up with both hands.

Walking Thoughts

The sidewalk is growing soft. I am growing soft.
Absence is a principle, a silence wholly.
If the moon fell, there would be no use for it.

What do we mean by "a killing effort?"
Back there, back there the darkness waits.
Everything we know is a circle.

In a dumb country, the one way is everyone's.
And something has a chance in such a land.
Is my last friend ahead under that light?

I walk on, and watchdogs bark crossly.
The other sidewalk is softening also.
It lets me down with curious consistency.

Settling for the average of full and empty
I turn toward home, begin to hurry in the dark,
have talked myself into going back once more.

The Hole in the Sea

It's there
in the hole of the sea
where the solid truth lies,
written and bottled,
and guarded by limp-
winged angels—
one word under glass,
magnified by longing
and by the light tricks
of the moving man
in the moon.
Nights, that word shows,
up from the bottle,
up through the water,
up from the imaginable.
So that all who cannot
imagine, but yearn toward,
the word in the water,
finding it smaller
in the hole in the sea,
rest there. If no one
has drowned quite
in the hole of the sea,
that is a point
for theology. "Blame God
when the waters part,"
say sailors and Hebrews;
blame God, who writes us,
from His holy solution,
not to be sunk,
though all our vessels
convey black messages
of the end of the world.
So goes the story,
the storybook story, so goes
the saleable story:
Courage is in that bottle,
the driest thing there is.

FROM

A Probable Volume
of Dreams

(1 9 6 9)

Give Back, Give Back

If I married him for length,
none was so little so long.
How think to explain it?—
Words I have known are now his,
his weight rests under my pillow.
I have nothing for floating.

My children are of groceries,
and not of love. None
has fallen for years, none come crying,
as if the middle years were trying
to break me of my light warping.
I am not so lucky for looking.

On the white sheet of his will
my children inherited
the objects of original pleasure, his
for which I gave up pleasure,
for pleasure, in pleasure, to pleasure.
I am the lot of him, as is my wont.

Yet have wanted to wear the ring of him,
hear it and recreate it.
Into the night those marriages go
to which woman is bound to be used.
All over I hear the breathing pause
at the long entrance of the children.

I'll Be There

The grass and the water receive me.
Into those vapors, love returns.

Into his closet, the lover's clothes
go to hang. His bones rattle
in that box in its shaft.

Wasn't it yesterday
he was wearing us out
with his tricks and his tastes
and his tinkering? Wasn't it yesterday
he was the "ardent but changeable"
lover in your future?

Just so, he would say,
but you wouldn't believe him.

Yet because he approached you
the moon turned into
the moon of you,
and because he approached you
the clear light walked.

When I am the knowledge of you,
can I ever be false? And

will you please, he never said,
look after Mother?

A Picture of Soldiers

They are doughboys, of doughboy bearing,
shot in the thick-soled brownshoes of trainees,
the high necks and wide brims to be foregone,
and the camp and company of that lost peace.

Here they affected their final rank and file,
from which they recovered to western fronts
to short the batteries of the Kaiser
and oppose the shockwaves of his troopers.

They advanced without water, with inadequate
supplies, they lost their weapons but drove on,
when they lost their arms they went without them,
and then without feet and without stomachs.

They dug into the Argonne, buried Belleau Wood,
planted the trenches of forests, seeded their faults;
they lay down at their funerals in those forests,
leaving issue and rations to remainder,

and this rifle-long photo for my study,
in which these soldiers-to-end-all-soldiers
give up their fathering, give to the living
the next invention, the next impossible President.

World War III

I
You post a sign,
"We have gone to the cellar to die."

Ready to descend,
you hear the motors of airplanes.

You look up to see
the American right wing.

You think of the euphemism for pay:
"This is the day the eagle craps."

II
All the planes are driven
by suicide pilots.

The young fliers are ready to drown,
to fill the oceans, if need be,

while the fish cough
on dry land.

Mountains will fill valleys,
the beaches fuse.

III
You decide against shelter.
Instead, you stand on your porch.

In the sun,
that old fireball,

you stand on your porch with your family.
You tell them not to worry.

It's a nice day, you say,
such warmth on your skin.

The Parents of Psychotic Children

They renounce the very idea
of information, they are enamored
of the notion of the white tablet.
Their babies were outrageously beautiful
objects exploding their lives,
moving without compensation
because of them to worlds without them.
They believe they were presented
inadequate safeguards, faulty retribution,
and a concerted retirement into crime
of the many intent on their injury.
No two can agree on the miraculous
by which they were afflicted,
but with economy overcome
their fears of the worst. Their children, alas,
request nothing. And the far-fetched doctors,
out of touch with the serious truth,
are just practical and do not sing,
like the crazy birds, to their offspring.

The Extermination of the Jews

A thousand years from now
they will be remembered as heroes.
A thousand years from now
they will still be promised their past.

Objects of beauty notwithstanding,
once more they will appear
for their ruin, seeking a purse,
hard bread or a heavy weapon

for those who must survive,
but no one shall survive.
We who have not forgotten,
our children shall outremember:

their victims' pious chanting—
last wishes, last Yiddish, last dreaming—
were defeats with which the Gestapo
continues ceasing and ceasing.

The War Piece

I
The dove has entered the hawk-farm,
the dove has entered the crows' nest.

He has flown on into the eagle-cage,
he has fallen in with the vultures.

The drone and the cuckoo have welcomed
the gull and the goose who have welcomed

II
the buzzard and locust and swallow.
The dove has landed in the fowl-coop.

The grasshopper can witness nothing;
and the owl and the catbird, nothing.

The rooster's voice is buried in light
and the moth, dying, buries the light.

III
The warblers have given up flying.
And the sparrows have given up flying.

Left, the pigeons are flying,
looking like last lost doves.

Their pigeon necks are next-to-last
under the bird-like and black, widow cloud.

FROM

The Escape into You
A Sequence

(1971)

A Biography

Poetry cripples. *Tempus fugit.*
Have removed from the lit'ry wars
the hand of a gentleman in quill,
the blackberry ink mixed with tears,
who sought the ingratitude of his day
as a sculptor, clay or an alchemist, brass.

Poet or poem? Life or art?
He cared for his judgments in their prisons,
he likened himself to a convict,
he lifted his vision to the window,
he dug for the treasures of light,
he entered the solitary's tunnel.

Women he loved he surrendered,
as leaf falls for the love of leaf.
Felons he insulted and readers perverted.
In the cave of the senseless, it all fit:
the thin shafts the stars shone down
could not lighten his life at hard labor.

Homage to the Runner

The form of this "sport" is pain,
riding up into it, he hurts to win.
These are the moments when death is really
possible, when a man can fit into
his enlarged heart all that is known
or was or shall be pumping fulfills.

The love of form is a black occasion
through which some light must show
in a hundred years of commitment.
By the time the body aches to end it,
the poem begins, at first in darkness,
surrounded by counterfeits of leisure.

Run away. Leave them to ease.
What does it matter you wind up alone?
There is no finish; you can stop for no one.
When your wife cries, you pass a kiss.
When your sons worry, you flash a smile.
When your women wave, you ignore them.

I Adore You (1960)

What to include?—I borrowed money
from you, rubber bands, like
a rubber band space in your bed, we
banded together. Turned out, forever.
Lust piece, collar and elastic,
I'm glad I was up to participate.

I took time off from work, wife
on the way out, took to you candy
flowers, bittersweet grounds for mid-
morning Mexican divorce stemming
adultery from. Living conditions improved
because receptive to my advances.

In all those pastorals, teetering sheep,
when the wooden lover stubs his
badly extended heart wanting mother.
Not us. Though my father was just dead,
Mother thought you an angel:
down from heaven, up for grabs.

The Escape into You

Eight years of making it, who deserves
that many more, like a reprieve
from war the weekend soldier
furloughs into a medal of dishonor?
It wasn't enough to be a mountain,
you had to be a river I couldn't swim.

We had your body to build on.
Even that arranged a little paranoia
like a face you almost once
recognized over a raincoat when
the elements came together, you
swearing, what a gasp to see an old friend.

A slut could have broken my heart,
the way we lived. The event, for all that,
was so special I never asked, Are you,
or are you not, overcome by my fast
glandular diabolism, huh? Soldiers
leaped; I loved your silent stones.

1968

A Memory

The first wife floats in memory calmly
who formerly was storm-tossed, who gave
at the edges a whitewash to those rocks
on which she would founder, who founded
the Territory Hysteria, bordering
the knife, the state of the doomed union,

who spent lavishly the genital coin,
who ate up the year's best and its worst,
who was the slaveship that came in,
who wasted the fortune in the hold we
have mentioned, who put out for history
a veil of tears, and a sour milk steam.

Recall, also, how you arrived by that ship,
seasick and blubbering as much as anyone,
and how it took you, for all its wooden groans,
to land, and then let you leave.
You were the dullest coxswain alive.
You were put in the hole for good reason.

Homage to Alfred Stieglitz

The address of the equivalent
is in the cloudy mind though also
"out there." You must face it.
One bush, a thousand faces.
So there is also camera-work in love.
So there is also work.

But the mind wants to dwell on the body.
In New England, in winter, in long ago,
the faces of evil
were seen, severally, by hard-working
settlers though cold suited them.
The truth would set them on fire.

Once, in a field of vision,
we were acting without persistence,
and in a room with one light let
the buffeted optics of beauty
into my camera. The idea was dizzying:
I could never expose you enough.

Honi Soit Qui Mal Y Pense

*Meta*physical, not pornography,
to say we balanced each other.
Some thought it bad to exercise
unless trying to have children.
If we had a thousand, it wouldn't
be enough but just crowded.

On a lonely isle, you are
my idea. In a slow dream of going
across China, you are company.
But still I don't love you
because I have no choice.
I love your voice

saying nothing but moans,
no eyes, no moons: pushing the black
back by the virtues of your sex,
which are those parts of you—
heart but one, and that figurative—
I enter into I love.

Rescue, Rescue

I need you like a sailor needs
his hardtack, I have floundered
far from shore away from paradise,
I need you to cut my teeth on.
It's not easy to let you loose,
not to set you up so I'll need you.

I need you when the boat rolls,
when the mast we thought an arrow
snaps; I swim like a stone.
If you're free, I'm over here,
and over here!, and over here!
The better you swim, the more I drown.

I have worried if the lungs can survive
these extra washings, if the heart
won't wrinkle and the hands retract.
What I've given I wouldn't take back.
I wanted something perfect; without me,
the rescues succeed without regrets.

Light Poem

I'm in a phone booth in Saratoga Springs.
The water tastes awful, but very helpful.
You aren't answering, whatever I'm asking.
I'm asking right now why you aren't answering.
It's pleasure, pain, or just love of quiet.
You're not answering; I've got coins for nothing.

I'm going to stamp out my feelings for you,
post them in a letter like a long shaft
brought to your box by fanjet airlines.
On a plain chair, arms flapping, I'm winging
to that heaven of babies, that stellar
interstellar galaxy of persuasions, those

fine passions eclipsed by sunshine
but now, in the dark, all that we see
and all that we ever wished for, swore for,
lied and cheated and stole for.
I'm sending you tomorrow the letter of today,
a little dried-up light from far away.

Your Shakespeare

If I am sentenced not to talk to you,
and you are sentenced not to talk to me,
then we wear the clothes of the desert
serving that sentence, we are the leaves
trampled underfoot, not even fit to be
ground in for food, then we are the snow.

If you are not what I take you to be,
and I am not what you take me to be,
then we are the glass the bridegroom smashes,
the lost tribes underfoot, no one sees,
no one can speak to us, in such seas we
drift in we cannot be saved, we are the rain.

If I am unable to help myself,
and you are unable to help yourself,
then anything will happen but nothing follows,
we eat constantly but nothing satisfies.
We live, finally, on the simplest notions:
bits of glass in the head's reticent weather.

The Making Way

The husband's ribs like the tree
you might have lived under
give you protection everything comes through
whether solace or mercy,
whether relation of blood or word of mouth.
The ear is oppressed to be so cared for.

The crickets sing their rounds endlessly
until someone approaches.
Then, in the silence, there comes to say
There is an end to the random,
a moment which requires your departure.
You press your seal of goodbye against him.

O what will he do with small children,
or with no one to keep his company?
That's not what he affords
by letting you go, but bountiful harvest.
He doesn't fall, but bends a little;
he gives you a way to the light.

From the Wardrobe

Collecting hearts, drawing you out—
like the billowy message the pulleys
whined between ledges, for which
you stood undressing, for which no one
objected long to showing the tongue so—
I shuck the thick skin just by talking,

sometimes. But sometimes the clothesline
sags with labor and lucklessness—
the faded house prints, the making-do—
and you see in these tenements nothing
of the young girl whose hair was a river
her lover set sail on, and out from.

And if the sails are sooty sheets now,
and if the pulleys creak to go nowhere,
what is that on the ocean?
The woman abandoned is an old story
the gulls will not feed on.
Every so often, you must dress it up.

We Have Known

We have known such joy as a child knows.
My sons, in whom everything rests,
know that there were those who were deeply
in love, and who asked you in,
and who did not claim a tree of thoughts
like family branches would sustain you.

My sons, in whom I am well pleased,
you will learn that a man is not a child,
and there is that which a woman cannot bear,
but as deep wounds for which you may hate
me, who must live in you a long time,
coursing abrasively in the murky passages.

These poems, also, are such and such passages
as I have had to leave you. If very little
can pass through them, know that I did,
and made them, and finally did not need them.
We have known such joys as a child knows,
and will not survive, though you have them.

Vision doesn't mean anything real
for most of them. They dance
beautifully way out on the thin limbs
at the top of the family tree,
which we have admired for
its solid trunk and unseen roots

we know go back to other countries
where "God help us" was a prayer
one planted like a seed, staking everything
on labor, luck and no concessions.
All of us remember the rains that year
which exhausted the Czar and the Bolsheviks.

Hungry, wet, not yet sick of ourselves,
we escaped by parting the waters;
we brought this black bread to live on,
and extra enough for a child.
That bread didn't grow on trees.
We multiplied, but we didn't reproduce.

The Einstein Poems

Fall, and the sick elms pour themselves
into themselves: funnels for DDT, passage-
ways for the fallen, alms for the poor.
Where once there were robins, dry rot;
where there were beds, misery's company.
The legacy's writ large in Railroad Gothic:

a funereal invitation a spider's patience
could not have knotted in the lushest garden
except he stitched it through his own bowels.
Fly into that web; it will gut him.
In that deep cave, love's a last meal
you will never wash your mouth of.

You would eat flowers if the flowers were
healthy, you would dine on the sidewalks
if the concrete had some specific purpose,
you would flush your insides if the water
were holy, you would love your neighbor
if he would help you help it help him.

On Utilitarianism

Everyone wants to feed everyone else.
Piled in back alleys, bread greens
antibiotics of its soft centers,
money foments yeast reaching the moon,
change turns into silverfish kids drop
gum for. We cast it on *these* waters.

We turn rubber into trees, flowers,
make a cow of loose leather, a sow's ear
of a ruined purse, we change wine to blood,
bread into flesh, as if there were no tomorrow
we change men into women, alter the course
of the stars, we try to beat the odds.

The odds remain; the chances come and go.
Peace in the backwoods is deep in that nature
we long since baptized and confessed to
we wanted out. Now that we are free of the woods,
we try making that forest for the future
in the city where there's no tomorrow.

Getting Lost in Nazi Germany

You do not move about, but try
to maintain your position. Would you eat
the fruit of the corpses?—You would.
Your friends are the points of a star
now a golden, unattainable "elsewhere"
because there is no elsewhere for a Jew.

Men have closed their daughters to you,
and now the borders like neat hairlines
limiting your ideas to hatred and escape.
This way, they have already begun
the experiments with your brain—
later to be quartered and posted.

Cremation of what remains?
In a dream like this one, a weathered face
will drive you off under a load of hay
at the very moment the Commandant calls.
You could swear the voice you hear is kind,
calling you home, little Jewboy in alarm.

The Children

The death of the father is my shepherd,
he maketh me three versions of wanting.
He giveth back my shadow; he restores.
He pays out and pays out the darkness.
How much does it cost to keep silence?

How much does it cost to keep calm?
It costs my brother his heart like a sleeve.
It costs for the children with no hearts.
It costs in the stomach, when it is kicked in,
on the flaming arms of the infants,
jelly to jelly it costs in the mother's ovaries.

We are the just gypsies dictators hate.
We contain the hate and wrap it in a warm
blanket of babyfat, while the bones
wait in the children's graveyard at the Capitol.
Or here they come walking!, hands joined by chains,
on the cobbled *Calle de Niños Heroes*.

If their rags embarrass you, will you wipe your noses?

3 Stanzas about a Tree

1 : The tree, too, wants to bend over
and wait a million years for an agate bridge
itself may have become, as we
turn and turn into, with final grace,
that seamless singleness we could not embody
across the river in our own bodies.

2 : The tree has bent over which carried
us here, striations like glyphs from
who-could-imagine, and there were plenty,
too, who came for the sun,
who now are burnt into the earth
in a black seal familiar to but one or two.

3 : Have we a vault for fury, a cathedral,
like the redwood? Have we wanted to be glass
or a diamond of the first water? That oak
has the same date with carbon we have.
Have I (think!) wanted to be the tree, or
one, two or three stanzas about a tree?

What Lasts

So help me, Love, you and I.
Paper into pulp, and our words last
as ashes to cool the sun.
The pen lasts in stories by the fire,
the ink bubbles, the word is cremated
and spreads dumbly as in our lungs.

I wanted to speak it now. And how
the explosive sound of the lungs,
collapsing as they give back air—
we have had that energy, burning.
We have been at the throat of the world.
We have had a lifetime.

I concede to that blue flower, the sky,
a more than passing moral guidance.
Because light flashes, dies, flashes,
some sing the rhapsody of the liver.
Yet what the symbol is to the flower
the flower itself is to something or other.

The Defeat of the Intellect

We have boxed it into a corner, where
it snarls and writhes in a terrible odor
burning rubber could not cover.
It hates us, in its furry outer logic,
as a child hates its father
in guilt, for guilt, when it is time to.

Now it is time to fly at the center,
to become the arrow. We will feather
the eye of the target, enlightenment
like a jar of fireflies for keeping
small worlds lit. They are like white
pills, the chaste ladies of fast fortune;

the light we can divide and conquer.
But there is another light, beyond
the jar, the shining bodies, the world
we can say, it surrounds the love we
do not luggage, like an Egypt full of
Jews it makes no sense.

Constant Feelings

Some acts I could never, not
forthrightly, not by flanking
you, accomplish, like that bridge
the poet tried to put in his poem
to be put in his pocket (another
became a bearskin, already shed).

I wanted to harp on that bridge,
of course to be that bluebottle, corn-
flower, the three leaves of the sassafras.
Naturally I hoped the coat of my arms
would, when I reached for you, spin off,
revealing the new skin of a purer animal.

I think I shall always love you.
When I enter your skin, I am closer
to bear, bridge, bush and that tree
which, granting the lovers shade,
will be my veins round yours: many loves
which are lives, but do not depend on lives.

Song: The Organic Years

Love, if nothing solid rises like wood
above this scratching, this waxen cane
of a tree, if nothing from this trunk
unflowers after long reaching, if finally
the leaf relaxes its bodily processes,
at least we had a hand out to help it.

Also, you have carried me far on your
way into the earth, in the prophetic
imagery of your tunnels I was satisfied,
and in your lovely arms I lay weeping
the truth. If belief doesn't make up
for the long argument of life, still

we made up with what was natural. Now,
from the long, blind alleys of learning,
and in the winter of metaphor, our arms
reach like branches toward the light, our
roots go down to clear water, our fingers,
so long counted on, are not dry yet.

The Willing

I am not yet ready to die inside,
while the ash founds a society of its own
rooted in the clean dirt, while
the berry tree signals its neighborliness
and the weeping willow says "forgive."

Mister of the chapel, Mister of the steeple,
who says go there when the road is a ladder?
I have to take that promise myself
which ended for so many without flowering
and sit the branches and the buds through

storm of birth, whipping of circumstance,
lacerations like birthdays in the garden.
Surely foliage needs this beating of foliage
to aspire to: the winds effacing the trees,
the open spaces up ahead pleasing danger.

Obsessive

It could be a clip, it could be a comb;
it could be your mother, coming home.
It could be a rooster; perhaps it's a comb;
it could be your father, coming home.
It could be a paper; it could be a pin.
It could be your childhood, sinking in.

The toys give off the nervousness of age.
It's useless pretending they aren't finished:
faces faded, unable to stand,
buttons lost down the drain during baths.
Those were the days we loved down there,
the soap disappearing as the water spoke,

saying, it could be a wheel, maybe a pipe;
it could be your father, taking his nap.
Legs propped straight, the head tilted back;
the end was near when he could keep track.
It could be the first one; it could be the second;
the father of a friend just sickened and sickened.

Put Back the Dark

Let's not stop in cold, in drought,
but blanket and seed our own bed.
We'll be a long time dead.
We walk now on stilts, on dagger heels,
through the howling of impatience
and the ailing imprisoned.

We walk now through the jails,
nothing to provide, a notion of being
free leading us from these helpless,
away from ambition and vanity,
toward the comfort of solitude
like a tree living two-thirds in death.

There is nothing left to resist,
where there is nothing irresistible.
So these poor cities fade from vision
not maniacally but as an old memory
which was not important to that dream
when your hand into mine put back the dark.

FROM

Residue of Song

(1 9 7 4)

The Hurt Trees

1
These are bit black flowers
on a scruffy winter plane:
a pure mid-country poetry.

Heaven has come down to earth
like rain to dry crackers,
in fact as sleet to these branches,

like: chance, functioning with elegance.
The dead leaf and the globe
and our elastic yearnings

wind in the mind around limbs
which we call "fingers,"
or "heaven," that goal for cows.

2
And we put life into stones.
Without us, stones have already
the still lives of stones,

but we are not satisfied.
To float a stone,
to obtain the key,

the sense of the stars taking
their positions, the fullness
of the earth come round,

one day away
from the duplicate repertoires,
we would have given our lives.

3
For a line inside, for
one line from inside,
we furnish these passages, these

honeycombed catacombs so far from light
the stars offer their past,
these mind-corridors with their

worst that is not over,
and their own stones, and own winters,
their strung trees.

4
And there was a highway!
A large stone on the road
meant something around the curve.

Your death left you for a moment.
A heavy foot kicked you from behind.
Do you speak English, eh?—

because what you see will be foreign
to you, and foreign to nature,
but made by nature nonetheless:

a man in pain,
a woman in pain,
an accident of nature.

5
And it is wholly an accident
that you were ever there to see it
in that country you summered in,

long before,
before the winter that hurt the trees
and made your eyes water.

Residue of Song

You were writing a long poem, yes,
about marriage, called "On Loneliness."
Then you decided not to.
There was a certain inconsolable *person*.
You felt you had to discover who.
You would be shocked to discover it was
not yourself. Yourself!, yourself!,
as if the whole world were but glass
for your splendid insights, put softly.
Who was it walked the length of the lawn,
crossed over into a brilliance you knew came
from another world, but from where?
She was out walking, and you were afraid for the children!
Had she taken out a knife? Had she
pledged her return though nothing changed?
Had she even realized how *wilful* all this was:
hysteria, dry heaving, the throat crawling
with sounds ground down from expectation,
because you lied to her about—was it
other women? No. Because you told the truth,
of course that was a kind of weeping
as if unto Mother, for approval and pointers.
Yes, yes, you expected understanding
and refreshed company, since you were the lonely.
It was as if you had been waiting on the corner,
with who knows what exploits seemingly on your lapels,
when *she* walked by: not forked prey, but a friend!
You brought her your past; she wept.
She brought you her future; you mislaid it,
later you squeezed until it uttered, *piano*,
"Where are we? Where, for that matter, were we
when we met? I was out walking, and you,
coming from shadow, postured like the children
we agreed upon. Amidst wickedness, we were the age,
if the age was wicked, but safe on the surface.
Suddenly, we were responsible for discourse, whereas,
years earlier, we had been held only by the moon.
What did you tell the others then, over your shoulder,

calling me to stop you—that you would never?
One appointment leads to another in these soft days.
A photograph of flowers the skin remembers,
a bowl of leaves before the kitchen screen,
is to this life as you are to mine. Your cries,
for ecstatic madness, are not sadder than some things.
From the residue of song, I have barely said my love again,
as if for the last time, believing that you will leave me."

Temper

The seed, in its grave,
is the firmest line of labor.
A man woos havoc to undertake
the destruction of a dam in a drought.

Weren't you wound up to be metal
rulers for the hocus-pocus?
The great face of the earth
is pained to be nothing without you:

a sopping interdependence
to make bricks from mud and a family
from seed, and anger
clear through to the center.

The Price Is Right

They turned over the wrong card but then
the right card and the girl won two motorcycles.
She can ride them one at a time or
both together, and her husband if she has one
can go on ahead in the family car.
We've come so far on the wheel we can't
look back for fear of falling, though one man
survived a crash that I know of. Some of you might
remember the plane that fell in Brooklyn,
from which a burning child was the only survivor
but died in shock a day later. If you can't
talk about it without throwing up, there's
some hope for you but no future.

Aristotle

He put in their places as much as he had time for,
and though the word for this is missing
in its entirety we know he knew how it feels
when the hurt and humiliation defeat
guts and gravity to come up out of us
shouting about art instead of murder and giving
to pain the high-sounding name of "tragedy"—
which is a fall from a high place by a weak
sister; *i.e.*, you can jump from a skyscraper
and learn nothing from doing.

Being in Love

with someone who is not in love with
you, you understand my predicament.
Being in love with you, who are not
in love with me, you understand my dilemma.
Being in love with your being in love
with me, which you are not, you understand

the difficulty. Being in love with your
being, you can well imagine how hard it is.
Being in love with your being you,
no matter you are not your being being in
love with me, you can appreciate and pity
being in love with you. Being in love

with someone who is not in love, you know
all about being in love when being in love
is being in love with someone who is not
in love being with you, which is
being in love, which you know only too well,
Love, being in love with being in love.

Here

on Venus, time passes slowly because
we are all preoccupied with love.
The trees build up like sponges,
the crust under us accumulates like coral,
we begin to feel the long pressure
the jewel feels, if the jewel feels,
and, although this is suspicious belief,
we welcome the illusion with that thrill
formerly reserved for the profane.
His hands are under her buttocks;
her legs are bent on his shoulders;
their extensions are the piping for
"the best that has been thought or said."
The image is of a brain for all space.
The universe, remember, is a ribbon
where we follow back to the beginning
and so meet that one of whom you were thinking
when you mistook being here for being there.

Little Father Poem

We must stay away from our fathers,
who have big ears. We must stay away
from our fathers, who are the snow.
We must avoid the touch of the leaves
who are our proud fathers. We must
watch out for father underfoot. Father
forgave us when we did nothing wrong,
Father made us well when we were healthy,
now Father wants to support us
when we weigh nothing, Father in his grave
gives us everything we ever wanted,
in a boat crossing who-knows-where,
mist flat over the water,
the sand smooth because soft.

To the Sky

in memory of H.R.

We are green with our haggard deities.
Yet we are each virgin fortress.

We are prayer like a net
beneath the story of fall.

We are stones asking stars.
We will be sweet dust.

You Would Know

thirteen poems to my father

1 *Origin of Dreams*

Out from muted bee-sounds and musketry
(the hard works of our ears, dissembling),
under steeply-held birds (in that air
the mind draws of our laid breathing),
out from light dust and the retinal gray,
your face as in your forties appears
as if to be pictured, and will not go away.

I have shut up all my cameras, really,
Father, and thought I did not speak to you,
since you are dead. But you last;
are proved in the distance of a wrist.
Your face in dreams sends a crinkly static
and seems, in its mica- or leaf-like texture,
the nightworks of the viscera.

But feeling's not fancy, fancying you.
I don't forget you, or give stinks for thanks.
I think I think the bed's a balcony,
until we sleep. Then our good intentions
lower us to the dead, where we live.
I think that light's a sheet for the days,
which we lose. Then we go looking.

2   *If You Lived in Moscow*

We've got the morning—that much
we still have, no thanks to the Tsar.
If you lived in Moscow, you'd appreciate
those black cauldrons they melt the snow in—
the dirty snow only, doing the sun's work.
The Russian white acacia's also American:
our hard black locust, straight to the boatyard!

You had its drugs and gums and cures,
and had cucumber seeds to cool passions!,
but it's that acacia that still interests me.
Is this because a wounded man
cut trees from paper, and made in this way
for himself a sacred wood? I do remember
in your town the kids picked up the corpses.

He, him, his—used by us of the enemy
at all times. Even more so, formerly.
For now the lonely poet resents
any imitation of his and his father's
past happiness, in a boat or on the shore.
Your Russia, without you, is cold and desolate,
of difficult access and of no importance.

3   *Father and Russia*

I see you by thin, flighty apple trees,
picking fruit out of the branched air,
find you in a hand of ice, of which one-third
only appears to welcome but forbid at once.
No, it was only more snow I saw, freezing
completely the fists and fingers of the fruit trees.
You had no intention to smile away your orchard.

Mother Russia's iron militia's a monster,
the thunder of Cossack horses
is a long storm you lip-read the Tsar by.
Your mother knuckles the washboard into your teens,
but plans your escape. Your father sends money.
You in your orchard still fill the wooden baskets,
while the too-long-perfect bruise and fall.

Now I want you as you were before they hurt you,
irreparably as you were as in another country.
The harvest moon, sunset's clockwork, can show us
what to pick, but not whom to pick on.
Step here with me, and stay, and blame the birds
whose unschooled bedlam in the sweltering cherries
is all the blame and harm a tree can bear.

4   *Who Killed Christ?*

The square is as high and as wide
as a man with his arms outstretched.
The Hebrew letter is blasphemous
to a Christian world. In a Christian world,
the blasphemous Hebrew letter
is the name of God, and the name of God
is like unto the name of the Father,

Father. Every man will be a tree,
may become a shaft stars rain down.
"He-who-labored" came unto me
and I gave him rest: in seeds, pools and poems,
I pardoned the water for no man
can swim in the channel, I let the father
assume all the shapes of the tides,

and I stood against the forsaken beaches
and cried to say something to insult you.
Now the children are scared of the beast-face
at the window, and the window fears cold.
Unless I miss my guess, the plants too
have their feelings, the animals don't worship,
so I stand here looking out for no one.

5   *Letting in Cold*

Who killed Christ?—my favorite subject.
You misunderstood my love for Russia,
going so far you changed love into hate,
which was not my intention. You know,
in your time you changed life into death,
what-is to what-is-not, schooling to recess.
The enigmatic lesson in geography! that

wasn't the teacher's way of instructing
but only my way of trying propriety.
The proper study of man is where he came from!
You came from Russia—under the hayloads,
bareback to Poland, steerage to America.
The tip of the whip the teacher withdraws
comes all the way from a bitter Europe.

Today, here, the first new snow
bothers the softness in people, and they are kind.
In four months, the world will seem harsh
as ever, a localness, a locking-out that continues,
and we will stand corrected, half-dead and
corrected. No one approaches the father's thoughts
where he stands, at the back door, letting in cold.

6   *Following*

Your eye at the glass proves snow
falling now for an unseen hour.
Depth is all. We waited for Christmas.
Two Island ducks would stuff us.
We'd nap it off, then scavenge the birds.
One done wishbone would not suffice,
nor one wish, granted, fill us.

The rain that rose and fell, rose until
it changed to hail: those stones were large,
injurious, but we thought "marbles."
As in a pantry one thought of spicedrops,
and thought, too, the *kchunk* of the pump
a linking of water to water. One wanted to.
When I was there when you were there,

I wanted to. I also could fancy
that if one thing were like another
your being there was like your not being there,
if I paid attention. It was hard to follow.
Our house was a playhouse. You were my father.
The scattershot of ice, the chain-making of a pump,
were the rising sounds of your falling, better thought-of.

7   *Garlic*

Russian penicillin—that was the magic
of garlic, a party and cure. Sure,
you'll wrestle the flowers for fixings,
tap roots and saw branch for the ooze
of health, but you'll never get better.
I say you're living a life of leisure,
if life is life and leisure leisure.

The heart's half a prophet; it hurts
with the crabapple floating on top,
it aches just to know of the ocean—
the Old Country split off from the New—
and the acts of scissors inside you.
The heart of the East European,
poor boiler, is always born broken.

The sore heart weighs too much
for its own good. And Jewish health
is like snow in March, sometimes April.
The brothers who took their medicine
with you (garlic!) are dead now too.
The herb that beat back fever and sore
went home to its family: the lilies.

8   *From a Distance*

The tree will not ask for relief
though covered by sores and parasites
and misunderstood for a very long time.
Our shelled acorns and scalloped ivy,
our aromatic mint—trodden sentry—
are but underfooting for the wafer-
thin and hollow-needled snow

already bowing toward us under pressure
of a wet summer. An "early Iowa winter scene"
resembles a body, exquisitely blemished,
not lying but reclining as if modeling,
looking neither to the East nor the West,
and strangely! holding in place these shorn trees
we had passed by the mile without thankfulness.

But that is all changed. We lived on "the Island"—
New York's peninsular duck farm—
where the isolate fish-crow in the pine
gave a robber's thanks, and flew like a gash
through the air for the eggs of the others.
We were as far from the cities as I am from you,
which is not so far, Father, as you are from me.

9   *Demarcations*

The line between water and ice
is strychnine, a kind of nightshade.
The distance between the two of us, Father,
is poison, likewise time turned to substance,
as the first snow turns brief movements
between endless youth and unending age.
This white dust is everywhere!

This white dust everywhere is also
at the hooks of the quarter-moon this evening,
foretelling snow with a pompous emphasis.
Powder tumbles from the punctured capsule,
the peonies tuck and cower from harm,
the book of growth is closed,
and the man in winter bites down hard.

One summer I lived on the edge of, not in,
the Mad River. It was beautiful there, like trout,
and high class. Not like rainbow-less Ralston Creek
running brown past my winter house,
filling up on neighborhood knickknacks.
Elsewhere, I said that night was the distance.
This is the creek that travels that distance.

10   *The Thumb and One Finger Make Zero*

O, anything will do
to sink a song to you; I don't ask much.
Here's a glove, a factory "hand,"
encrusted fingers living in mold,
washed and pounded by snow for months,
now reaching from its elastic wrist
for all the world like someone buried.

Wherever's a pebble, there's a grave.
I go to work driving the gravel
that leads the dead here to highway.
Never blinding, it folds back the light
to the underworld, the rich dead.
You took some with you, and left lots more.
(And I was richer when you were poor.)

It's easy to miss you. I start for work,
maybe the roads "turn" into stairs,
the snowflakes placing their flat silence,
the clouds like faces refusing permission.
You see, it's winter. And much is covered.
But loss fits me like the gloves I leave.
I don't know where they turn up, or whether.

11   *Memorial Days*

He wears the weather; the grave is soft,
so soft I sink in old warnings:
"Walk on the dead; they'll walk in your head."
—Should I stay away? . . . or whistle.
So soft and drawn, so undergrown,
for now the sucking, heartless plot
could pass for flesh.

Memorials flash; I was the echo,
played second taps better than solo.
A little brave, far gone in the graveyard,
I ached the sweet cornet with sympathy;
then lingered, skipping the march for home.
How many were dead, and all at once?
—A child could wonder, whatever for.

My horn of plenty. I bled their hearts.
The granite markers gave me my measure,
and my directions. First, I shook sugar
out from those stones, waving the echo—
and whistled to stay the way I'd come
by cuts that led the polished stonecutters
to keep the untended, just within earshot.

12 *Trying to Catch Fire*

You go out when the sky is dark brown,
and the air is thick lotion,
though your son says the sky is still blue
(the son's job is to say it is the same).
You go out when the best drink on earth
is water, and the sun is a lion on fire
still, but gone from your sight and mind.

The son's job is to say the future
(maybe high blue will stand over us tomorrow).
When the sky is dark brown, you go out
and turn your thoughts to the bushes and your face
to the lithe tops of trees, whereas some
are stunted and some are twisted and then some
are old and wrinkled and they are perfect.

You stand close as possible to the perfect ones,
waiting for lightning. While you wait,
you worry an old saw: that the tree is "like"
a family, its branches to high heaven
(and there, blue luster or age's browning),
its roots sucking life from the dead. That's
a thought you can follow, inside, where you do.

You Would Know

13 You Would Know

That you, Father, are "in my mind,"
some will argue, who cherish the present
but flee the past. They haven't my need
to ask, What was I? Asking instead,
What am I?, they see themselves bejewelled
and wingèd. Because they would fly and have value,
their answers are pretty but false:

the fixings of facile alchemists,
preferring their stones to brains.
The brain, remember, is not foolproof
either, and does and does until it can't.
Sodden, quivering, crossed and recrossed,
the mind can become a headstone
or be malice stuffed with fish.

Everything changes so quickly. You who were
are no longer and what I was I'm not.
Am I to know myself, except as I was?
The rest is catchy, self-promising, false.
O please write to me, and tell me.
I just want to be happy again. That's
what I was, happy, maybe am, you would know.

78

Previously Uncollected

Study Guide for the *Odyssey*

1
Briefly,
in ten years what happened

before the story begins?
What does "odyssey" mean?

Identify Scylla and Charybdis.
Is this an epic?

Why ten years of war,
three of adventure

and seven with Calypso?
Is this an epic? Aristotle:

the romantic is wonderful
rather than probable.

2
Is there usually a feast or two,
a hero upon whom etc.,

a plea to the Muse for help?
Does Penelope handle her suitors?

What is an epithet?
Who lied—Odysseus or Homer?

Do we admire a trickster?
Is it hot where you lie reading

and are you aroused?
What does form "imitate"

and how?
Are you still beautiful?

3
Do you know a figure of speech
when you meet one?

Is it too far to you by now?
Is not this an epic

in which you have been lost?
Is Penelope so unlike Odysseus?

Trees Standing Bare

Those that do are not ashamed
to stand without leaves through the winter.
They know that loneliness
is not a clover pasture
or a stand of oak and hickory. They know
that the green of a pine
is all we will know of green,
and that all we will know of the dark
is sleep's forgetfulness.

Where He Stood: A Photographer's Portfolio

The Iowa land rolls and turns like the human body. Surprise, California! Surprise, New York! You out there have giants among you, mountains and skyscrapers to point to heaven. We have a flower in the moonlight, a river that goes black, a park's worth of trees that form up like a herd of cows, a silence the high winds pass without disturbing. We have a meadow of ivory, what snow turns to in our own gray. We have a spindly aspen on which every leaf is a message. We have a lacy weaving in the winter and a thaw in the spring you can see coming. The work gets done in the morning and the afternoon. Anything you say can go to find its echo, and love can go a long way where any eye can reach the horizon.

Because a tree is more important if you only have one. Because undulation is a slow movement in the mind that sees the land underfoot, not just a crossing. Because less is still more, three better than four, one over two.

Composition is something. We can ask where the photographer stood, but not why. Recognition is more of it, and subsumes composition. What do we recognize in the wordless world where we seek, inevitably, ourselves? Why take it down? Where did the photographer stand?

Time comes into it, may be all of it. A place may have a certain look three minutes a year, all things going one way. It will do no good to go over and over it. Those images which arrive, arrive at once. Words work another way, but have told of it. Emily Dickinson wrote, "There's a certain Slant of light," and found the sense it made: ". . . internal difference,/Where the Meanings, are."

These landscapes are different from many: little anthropomorphization, not much blatant mirroring, tones of gradation given an importance beyond forms, usually a levelling plane visible from here to there. Much is silvery, crystalline.

The curved eye wants to fit into the sky. Even in the snow, even in the water. It's a Midwest low-line, a report heading toward belief. Outside. Apart. Alone. Not lonely.

So you know where we stand.

84

FROM

Stars Which See,
Stars Which Do Not See

(1 9 7 7)

The Self and the Mulberry

I wanted to see the self, so I looked at the mulberry.
It had no trouble accepting its limits,
yet defining and redefining a small area
so that any shape was possible, any movement.
It stayed put, but was part of all the air.
I wanted to learn to be there and not there
like the continually changing, slightly moving
mulberry, wild cherry and particularly the willow.
Like the willow, I tried to weep without tears.
Like the cherry tree, I tried to be sturdy and productive.
Like the mulberry, I tried to keep moving.
I couldn't cry right, couldn't stay or go.
I kept losing parts of myself like a soft maple.
I fell ill like the elm. That was the end
of looking in nature to find a natural self.
Let nature think itself not manly enough!
Let nature wonder at the mystery of laughter.
Let nature hypothesize man's indifference to it.
Let nature take a turn at saying what love is!

The Poem

Would you like me more
if I were a woman?
Would you treat me better
were I a man?
I am just words, no
not words even, just marks
on a page, tokens of what?
Oh, you know.
Then tell them, will you.
Tell them to stop looking for me.
Tell them I never left home.
Tell them, if you must,
that I never left my body.
Unlike so many others,
I had no wings, just shoulders.
I was, like the snow bunting,
of stout build but moderate size.
Better make that "exceedingly" moderate size.
I neither blessed nor cursed
but that the good suffered
and evil closed the books in triumph.
I cured no one.
When I died, my bones
turned to dust, not diamonds.
At best, a tooth or two became coal.
How long it took.
You would have liked me then,
had you been alive still.
Had you survived
the silliness of the self,
you would have treated me better.
I never lied to you,
once I had grown up.
When x told you you were wonderful,
I said only that you existed.
When y said that you were awful,
I said only that life continues.
I did not mean a life like yours.

Not life so proud to be life.
Not life so conscious of life.
Not life reduced to this life or that life.
Not life as something—to see or own.
Not life as a form of life
which wants wings it doesn't have
and a skeleton of jewels,
not this one of bones and becoming.
How perfect are my words now,
in your absence!
Ungainly yet mild perhaps,
taking the place of no field,
offering neither to stand in the place of a tree
nor where the water was,
neither under your heel nor floating,
just gradually appearing,
gainless and insubstantial,
near you as always,
asking you to dance.

The Mystery of Emily Dickinson

Sometimes the weather goes on for days
but you were different. You were divine.
While the others wrote more and longer,
you wrote much more and much shorter.
I held your white dress once: 12 buttons.
In the cupola, the wasps struck glass
as hard to escape as you hit your sound
again and again asking Welcome. No one.

Except for you, it were a trifle:
This morning, not much after dawn,
in level country, not New England's,
through leftovers of summer rain I
went out rag-tag to the curb, only
a sleepy householder at his routine
bending to trash, when a young girl
in a white dress your size passed,

so softly!, carrying her shoes. It must be
she surprised me—her barefoot quick-step
and the earliness of the hour, your dress—
or surely I'd have spoken of it sooner.
I should have called to her, but a neighbor
wore that look you see against happiness.
I won't say anything would have happened
unless there was time, and eternity's plenty.

Trinket

I love watching the water
ooze through the crack in the fern pot,
it's a small thing

that slows time
and steadies
and gives me ideas of becoming

having nothing to do
with ambition or even reaching,
it isn't necessary at such times

to describe this,
it's no image for mean keeping,
it's no thing that small

but presence.
Other men look at the ocean,
and I do too,

though it is too many
presences for any
to absorb.

It's this other,
a little water, used, appearing
slowly around the sounds

of oxygen and small frictions,
that gives the self
the notion of the self

one is always losing
until these tiny embodiments
small enough to contain it.

Stars Which See, Stars Which Do Not See

They sat by the water. The fine women
had large breasts, tightly checked.
At each point, at every moment,
they seemed happy by the water.
The women wore hats like umbrellas
or carried umbrellas shaped like hats.
The men wore no hats and the water,
which wore no hats, had that well-known
mirror finish which tempts sailors.
Although the men and women seemed at rest
they were looking toward the river
and some way out into it but not beyond.
The scene was one of hearts and flowers
though this may be unfair. Nevertheless,
it was probable that the Seine had hurt them,
that they were "taken back" by its beauty
to where a slight breeze broke the mirror
and then its promise, but never the water.

Two Pictures of a Leaf

If I make up this leaf
in the shape of a fan, the day's cooler
and drier than any tree. But if
under a tree I place before me
this same leaf as on a plate,
dorsal side up and then its ribs
set down like the ribs of a fish—
then I know that fish are dead to us
from the trees, and the leaf
sprawls in the net of fall to be
boned and eaten while the wind gasps.
Ah then, the grounds are a formal ruin
whereon the lucky who lived
come to resemble so much that does not.

Acceptance Speech

My friends,
I am amazed

to be Professor
in a University

seven times larger
than my home town

and all because
I went away. Meanwhile,

the roots of the ivy
just went on crawling

in the dirt in the dark,
the light that was Brady's

and Gardner's during
our Civil War

became the blaze
in Southeast Asia

and soon everywhere
men lay down

without their women
which is what can happen

when people like me
leave home hoping

to be promoted
and end up promoted

to the rank of Captain
and discharged honorably

just before
whatever new war

we should always have known
was always coming

out of torn pockets and salt
from needles and patches of flowers

out of places for lost birds
night fog and a dying moon

from the work we do yea
(death being

what we don't do).
So to be at work

offending death
which others welcomed

who left home too
and no differently

seems to me half
of a famous story

I have never read
even in school.

To No One in Particular

Whether you sing or scream,
the process is the same.
You start, inside yourself,
a small explosion, the difference
being that in the scream
the throat is squeezed so that
the back of the tongue
can taste the brain's fear.
Also, spittle and phlegm
are components of the instrument.
I guess it would be possible
to take someone by the throat
and give him a good beating.
All the while, though, some fool
would be writing down the notes
of the victim, underscoring
this phrase, lightening this one,
adding a grace note and a trill
and instructions in one of those languages
revered for its vowels.
But all the time, it's consonants
coming from the throat.
Here's the one you were throttling,
still gagging out the guttural ch—
the throat-clearing, Yiddish ch—
and other consonants spurned by
opera singers and English teachers.
He won't bother you again.
He'll scrape home to take it out
on his wife, more bestial consonants
rising in pitch until spent.
Then he'll lock a leg over her
and snore, and all the time
he hasn't said a word we can repeat.
Even though we all speak his language.
Even though the toast in our throats
in the morning has a word for us—
not at all like bread in rain,

but something grittier in something
thicker, going through what we are.
Even though we snort and sniffle,
cough, hiccup, cry and come
and laugh until our stomachs turn.
Who will write down this language?
Who will do the work necessary?
Who will gag on a chickenbone
for observation? Who will breathe perfectly
under water? Whose slow murder
will disprove for all time
an alphabet meant to make sense?
Listen! I speak to you in one tongue,
but every moment that ever mattered to me
occurred in another language.
Starting with my first word.
To no one in particular.

A Fish: On Beauty

The catfish I'd caught was more whiskery
than whiskery, bigger than big enough.
The hammer that built the toolbox
was barely enough: it dotted its skull
like a cane impresses a carpet
and the blows repeated its life
half a dozen times before the end.

There was that detective in the story,
cornering the suspect, turned his revolver
in his hand and hammered the butt-end
against all protestations of innocence.
Artful, the way the author told it.
That catfish was ugly, I think.
The longer it took, the uglier he got.

After the Ducks Went In

We picked up eggs
and ducks. Some were sicker
than medicine, or the cost of it.
Weaklings, they lay on their sides.
They lifted their heads less and less.
Ducks are dumb
but even a duck has better sense
than to die. So I swung each
small contagion by its feet
against a tree till its neck broke.

I went far away to schoolroom *ethics*,
where too many were in
the lifeboat in the textbook.
Whom to toss out? The optimists
looked up everywhere, the pessimists
nowhere or down to let it happen.
Well, I could have broken my own neck
instead of those ducks'. Ethics
is not what you think.
Our class-conscience is clear. They all drowned.

Written During Depression: How to Be Happy

To be happy,
a man must love death
and failure. Then,
however great the flash
of this moment or that bit
of life's work, there
will come always another moment
to be appreciated because
fading or crumbling. If,
however, a man loves
life, there can be no end to it,
nor hope. If a man loves
reason, eventually he
will find none. If he loves
the interest of others,
he will be made to apologize
continually for his own being.
If he loves form, all
that he does or knows will
come, not to nothing, but
to that other possibility
of meaninglessness: everything.
That is why "the shape of things
to come" is a phrase littered with
tracks into the bush
where the pure primitive
is a headhunter's delusion,
and why, my dear, I love you.

Two Men in Wool Caps Catching Beaver

Home is a white sheet of a tent
strung to elms, and a stovepipe
come through up to an elbow.
From a peg where the door folds
a revolver hangs by its trigger guard.
Six skins are spaced along a line
while two fresh kills hang on a tree.

Sometimes, you think you know what people
think of you, and it's not much.
Then you have your picture taken.
Someone takes your photo in the sunlight
locking their elbows so that the trees
behind you come out sharp and even
the pleats at the corners of your eyes.

No one can say now you didn't laugh.
You were warm nights and kept by
a lantern. You knew how to preserve
whatever you wanted to save, lived on,
and protected your head. Now people
wear hats for looks, but yours had the
only style that matters: concern elsewhere.

An Elm We Lost

On it we wrote a little essay
about who loved who.
Shade moves in the grass, never still,
and they still do.

What Is There

When the grass, wet and matted,
is thick as a dry lawn is not,
I think of a kind of printing—
a page at a time, and the thick
paper hung up to dry, its
deep impressions filled and shapely
where ink is held and hardens.

And I wonder then at the underside
of those damp sheets of grass—
the muddy blood of those buried
coming up into the flattened green
as I press it underfoot, and pass,
and the sun drawing moisture
until we accept what is written there.

"Gradually, It Occurs to Us . . ."

Gradually, it occurs to us
that none of it was necessary—
not the heavy proclaiming
the sweat and length of our love
when, together, we thought it the end;
nor the care we gave your dress,
smoothing it as we would the sky;
nor the inevitable envelope of This-
is-the-time-we-always-knew-would-come,
and-goodbye. All that was ever needed
was all that we had to offer,
and we have had it all. I have your absence.
And have left myself inside you.
Now when you come back to me,
or I to you, don't give it a thought.
This time, when first we fall into bed,
we won't know who we are, or where,
or what is going to happen to us.
Time is memory. We have the time.

A Goldfinch

The Baltimore oriole, seldom an Iowan,
was last thought seen to be bathing
where we took coffee on a sweltering morning
yet in Iowa, a fan failing at our feet.
It was a sign, not of betrayal either.
That yellow breast of hers looked cool
and the white bars on her black wings
returned to us the formal in weather
without shape, shimmery. So a goldfinch.
The mind is a wonder, is my summary.

To Dorothy

You are not beautiful, exactly.
You are beautiful, inexactly.
You let a weed grow by the mulberry
and a mulberry grow by the house.
So close, in the personal quiet
of a windy night, it brushes the wall
and sweeps away the day till we sleep.

A child said it, and it seemed true:
"Things that are lost are all equal."
But it isn't true. If I lost you,
the air wouldn't move, nor the tree grow.
Someone would pull the weed, my flower.
The quiet wouldn't be yours. If I lost you,
I'd have to ask the grass to let me sleep.

Gemwood

to Nathan and Jason, our sons

In the *shoppes*
they're showing "gemwood":
the buffed-up flakes of dye-fed pines—
bright concentrics or bull's-eyes,
wide-eyed on the rack of
this newest "joint effort
of man and nature." But then

those life-lines circling
each target chip of "gemwood"
look less like eyes, yours or mine,
when we have watched a while.
They are more like the whorls
at the tips of our fingers,
which no one can copy. Even on

the photocopy Jason made of
his upraised hands, palms down
to the machine, they do not appear.
His hands at five-years-old—
why did we want to copy them, and
why does the gray yet clear print
make me sad? That summer,

the Mad River followed us
through Vermont—a lusher state than
our own. A thunderous matinee
of late snows, and then the peak
at Camel's Hump was bleached.
As a yellow pear is to the sky—
that was our feeling. We had with us

a rat from the lab—no, a pet
we'd named, a pure friend who changed
our minds. When it rained near
the whole of the summer, in that
cabin Nathan made her a social creature.
She was all our diversion, and brave.
That's why, when she died

in the heat of our car
one accidental day we didn't intend,
it hurt her master first and most,
being his first loss like that,
and the rest of our family felt badly
even to tears, for a heart that small.
We buried her by the road

in the Adirondack Mountains,
and kept our way to Iowa.
Now it seems to me the heart
must enlarge to hold the losses
we have ahead of us. I hold to
a certain sadness the way others
search for joy, though I like joy.

Home, sunlight cleared the air
and all the green's of consequence. Still
when it ends, we won't remember
that it ended. If parents must receive
the sobbing, that is nothing
when put next to the last crucial fact
of who is doing the crying.

FROM

These Green-Going-to-Yellow

(1 9 8 1)

These Green-Going-to-Yellow

This year,
I'm raising the emotional ante,
putting my face
in the leaves to be stepped on,
seeing myself among them, that is;
that is, likening
leaf-vein to artery, leaf to flesh,
the passage of a leaf in autumn
to the passage of autumn,
branch-tip and winter spaces
to possibilities, and possibility
to God. Even on East 61st Street
in the blowzy city of New York,
someone has planted a gingko
because it has leaves like fans like hands,
hand-leaves, and sex. Those lovely
Chinese hands on the sidewalks
so far from delicacy
or even, perhaps, another gender of gingko—
do we see them?
No one ever treated us so gently
as these green-going-to-yellow hands
fanned out where we walk.
No one ever fell down so quietly
and lay where we would look
when we were tired or embarrassed,
or so bowed down by humanity
that we had to watch out lest our shoes stumble,
and looked down not to look up
until something looked like parts of people
where we were walking. We have no
experience to make us see the gingko
or any other tree,
and, in our admiration for whatever grows tall
and outlives us,
we look away, or look at the middles of things,
which would not be our way
if we truly thought we were gods.

Haleakala Crater, Maui

I'm not going to reveal
the task I had, but it was big
and, as it should have been if
this is Life, beyond me.
I wanted something beyond me,
something the simple thought of which
shed night over all my reasons
and required of me more
than I required of myself,
something terrible, for one might talk
about it only to a lode of black
Godliness, such as one might come to
next to the blowhole of a volcano,
or take it unsaid to the psychical core-magnet
risen from lava and sulfur,
shepherd of cinder cone and crater,
sure in a hole in the clouds,
bottomless and wind-drawn,
mortal god immortal to men, there.
I walked. Or did not walk
but fought forward, wind-driven-back,
to take from that density
strength for a hard job coming.
It wasn't perfection I wanted,
with its need for form, hollow
unbroken shell, for all we know.
A place like this is different.
This is way beyond the social precepts
for which men have been flayed and women
turned inside out and flung down.
This is rock, massive, shocking,
lording over a green benevolence of fields,
unpromising, but absolutely
to be there.
Whoever has yet to be born
will understand me when I say that
I was once in a whistle
and I was once in a fish.

Haleakala Crater, Maui

And I was once in the center of the earth.
These were experience "beyond." And beyond these?
Beyond these is this heaviness
of the inner organs of a whole planet
spit-up to stay, powerfully
corresponding to our hard, twisted gut-ropes.

113

Someone Is Probably Dead

I

I already knew the secrets of light
before the snow.
It's the little light snowflakes—the dust,
not the pancakes—that make me crazy.
It's the little ones that make a blanket
of my coat and shut
out the stars and a chance to think.
Sometimes, there can be a blizzard where I stand
and nowhere else.
It's the same when a bright sun
in a hard sky
makes the plants in the window fuller.
I take it personally.
And even now, hiding from the snow,
just ten p.m., a Tuesday,
I sit under a green bursting indoors plant
with this feeling. The plant, surviving
nights I forgot to give it heat,
waterless weeks and a rough way
of doing business with it, all the time in its own way
picking off the red hairs of sunlight
and turning out succulent leaves that look like
skin on thick thumbs
or something worse—guts, maybe—manages. Doesn't
pilfer or make everyone around it miserable
against the day it will be picked up by one limp wing
and thrown down into the fly-infested trash.

2
Sometimes, I'll have been sick for three years,
but not with fever and thrashing
and the sheets torn round so that any doctor
would see at once a tight damp picture of illness.
No, sick with calm,
the catatonia of still beauty, the pretty prison
of memory, sometimes
just a face, just a name. It's a wonder
we're alive, we so much prefer the dead.

3
So once I took a ride in Chicago.
The cabbie's name was Purchase Slaughter.
He was all business. Not a star.
But a name that goes from here to there.
So I'm going to put him right here in front of you
and explain to you that when you drive
a taxi in the city for ten hours a day forever
you end up sitting perfectly still
and the city goes by you, turns right and left,
stops and starts up and you immobile
in your thoughts. Mr. Slaughter,
the anti-hero of these lines,
probably stands tonight in the snow off Lake Michigan
and curses the weather
which robs him of his income
and makes him live another life—or nothing.

4
It's stupid to pretend we can be someone else,
when someone else is dead.

Some Shadows

On the snow at night,
I saw once the shadow
of a huge sound,
which I had heard begin
as I passed under an old cherry tree,
then immaculate for winter.
There was the preparation,
which I can only say I heard,
though sound came next.
There was the sound, all at once—
a living thing, lifting.
I felt a giant presence
and looked down.
When I looked up, the shadow
I had seen leaving
took all the sky.
Too big for me,
I thought, but when I thought again
I could see again the owl
I had seen on the lawn of the church
the morning the Methodists
met to make the softball team.
Over its head, it wore
a number 3 paper bag.
Someone thought it could see better
in the dark. It
spoke a little, took a step
this way and that,
before someone else put it under an arm
and took it toward dusk.
I walked on the lawn
with the good Boy Scouts, thinking,
that dumb owl. Come out in the open
like that. I can see him today,
slowed by sunlight,
stuck to his shadow.
Inside the paper bag,
his pinned wing
made a sound like applause.

To an Adolescent Weeping Willow

I don't know what you think you're doing,
sweeping the ground. You
do it so easily, backhanded, forehanded.
You hardly bend. Really, you sway.
What can it mean
when a thing is so easy?

I threw dirt on my father's floor.
Not dirt, but a chopped green
dirt which picked up dirt.

I pushed the pushbroom.
I oiled the wooden floor of the store.

He bent over and lifted the coal
into the coalstove. With the back of the shovel
he came down on the rat just topping the bin
and into the fire.

What do you think?—Did he sway?
Did he kiss a rock for luck?
Did he soak up water
and climb into light and turn and turn?

Did he weep and weep in the yard?

Yes, I think he did. Yes,
now I think he did.

So Willow, you come sweep my floor.
I have no store.
I have a yard. A big yard.

I have a song to weep.
I have a cry.

You who rose up from the dirt,
because I put you there
and like to walk my head in under
your earliest feathery branches—
what can it mean
when a thing is so easy?

It means you are a boy.

Late Naps

There is a dead part of the day
when the soul goes away—the late afternoon,
for me, or else why is it
that sleep starts up in the stomach
in the late afternoons? The feeling,
like blood thinning-out up and across a gray
lining of stomach and intestines,
leads through moral disquiet to anxiety
to metaphysical alarm and then
sublime terror. Was anyone ever so scared?
Maybe you as the reader of this poem
can tell me: why can't the things one put back,
what one left behind, gave up on
or failed, keep their curses to themselves?
How is it that they who stand dumb in dream
know just when we are weakest,
and come again with their *if only*'s? You
tell me, I only know the bed
and the window and the blankets. I only know
the right side of the alarm clock,
and the paper cigarettes of the magazines
in the slim hands of the hazardous models
I take to my two pillows.
I only know the grain of that thing
that turns over and over in the mind
while the day turns
smoothly into the absolute cobalt of night.
And this happens even though,
like you, I took steps.
I left the Goddess' lava where it was,
I took nothing from the tombs.
I sent regrets, I left well enough. . . .
I know the dreamworks run on an oil so light,
it can be distilled from thin air.
In dreams, the sun is just a lamp,
and the soul—the soul is laughable,
putting on bedsheets or hovering in a cloud
of anesthesia with the melancholy eyes

of a wealthy schoolboy.
Some say the soul doesn't like to be taken
out of the body. Perhaps they're right,
for it gets nervous when the light fails.
It doesn't like getting dressed or flying.
It would like to just lie down and sleep for once,
leaving the ulcers to proxies,
and not wake up for a while.

A Motor

The heavy, wet, guttural
Small-plane engine
Fights for air, and goes down in humid darkness
About where the airport should be.
I take a lot for granted,
Not pleased to be living under the phlegm-
Soaked, gaseous, foggy and irradiated
Heavens whose angels wear collars in propjets
And live elsewhere in Clean Zones,
But figuring the air is full of sorrows.

I don't blame
The quick use of the entire earth
On the boozy
Pilot
Come down to get a dose of cobalt
For his cancer. He's got
A little life left, if
He doesn't have to take all day to reach it.
With the black patches
Inside him, and
The scars and the streaks and the sick stomach,

His life is more and more like
That of the lowliest child chimney sweep
In the mind of the great insensible,
William Blake. William Blake,
The repeated one, Blake, the half-mad,
Half-remembered,
Who knew his anatomy, down to
The little-observed muscle in the shoulder
That lifts the wing.

The little London chimney sweeper
Reaches up and reaches down.
In his back,
Every vertebra is separated from the long
Hours of stretching.

With one deep, tired breath,
The lungs go black.

By the Holiday Company crane,
Adding a level to the hospital,
On the highest land in the county,
Heavy sits the pure-white Air Care
Helicopter, with
Its bulging eye.
It has kept many going, a good buy,
Something.

Now someone I know says Blake
In anger,
Angry for his brother in the factory
And his sister on the ward,
But tonight I have no more anger
Than the muscle
That lifts my knee when I walk.

Another pleads with the ocean
That the words for
Suffering and trouble
Take place in a sound that will be all sounds
And in the tidal roll
Of all our lives and every event,
But I am silent by water,
And am less to such power
Than a failed lung.

And I think it is only a clever trick to know
That one thing may be contained
In another. Hence,
Blake in the sweep, one in the ground
In one in the air,
Myself in the clinic for runaway cells,
Now and later.

Letters from Africa

The self is small, and growing smaller.
But I write only: How are the children?
Every other day, in the morning,
while it is still the middle of the night for them,
I tell them I have awoken feeling fine.
By the time they read it I may be ill,
sick as a bony Moroccan dog
from a germ so utterly common
it needs no name.

But this moment I am well,
which makes me think they too are well,
and in six hours will also rise
and send their greetings also: *feeling fine.*
It is easier to write to them
if I imagine them awake.

Still, they sleep.
They do not hear my typing,
nor the sadness in my salutation:
Dear, uttered to three who sleep.
While there is time to decide what to write.

Does it matter that I looked for a letter,
that I have found a bookstore,
that I have changed my address? Or how the boys
felt four days ago across the ocean?
That it rains, and stops raining,
and rains again and the winds change direction?
No sails will bring my letters.
Will the date I put at the top matter
if we stay married? If we do not?

I place on a bench a bath towel, folded,
and the bench I place on a thick rug,
and the typewriter on the towel,
and I sit on the bed's edge and drink coffee
and write home, and never look up.

I have no view anyway. My window opens to
shutters, and the shutters to a stone wall,
white of course, with a lit window no one passes
though a bottle of water waits
half-empty on a small balcony. Why curtains
in a room with no view?
Dutifully, I open them mornings
and close them nights and at intimate moments,
to no end. No one can see, it seems
there is no one here who might want to,
no one who knows me knows that I am here,
and no one who sees me will know that it is I.

Yet if only because of this day,
I must think more about the light
that enters a room with no view,
and what I think is this:
As the light is no view, but better,
I am not here in this small room
and in these small details,
but abroad in the hearts of others,
even in other times
when I may have ceased to exist
but the last letter arrives without knowing.

Let me live now in the world without knowing.
The mustard grasses shine like thousands
of suns. The eucalyptus is statelier than I.
What good is it to be away
and not want to go home?

He Said To

crawl *toward* the machine guns
except to freeze
for explosions and flares.
It was still ninety degrees
at night in North Carolina,
August, rain and all.
The tracer bullets wanted
our asses, which we swore to keep
down, and the highlight
of this preposterous exercise
was finding myself in mud
and water during flares. I
hurried in the darkness—
over things and under things—
to reach the next black pool
in time, and once
I lay in the cool salve that
so suited all I had become
for two light-ups of the sky.
I took one inside and one
face of two watches I ruined
doing things like that,
and made a watch that works.
From the combat
infiltration course and
common sense, I made a man
to survive the Army, which means
that I made a man to survive
being a man.

In America

these things happen: I am taken
to see a friend
who talks too fast and is now teaching *Moby Dick*
according to jujitsu,
or judo according to Melville:
He says Melville gets you leaning
and lets go, or gets you to pulling
and suddenly advances, retreats
when you respond, and so on. Ok, I
accept that, but then he starts
in on the assassination of
John F. Kennedy as planned by our
government, and he has a collection of
strange deaths at handy times
bizarrely of people who know something.
I know nothing. I want to know
nothing whatsoever. It once
was enough to be standing
on a field of American baseball,
minding my ground balls and business,
when the infielder to my left
shot me the news of what is now known as
The Bay of Pigs, then in progress
but secretly, and certainly
doomed for stupidity, mis-timing,
marsh-landings, and JFK's resolve
to unaccomplish the Agency's *fait accompli*
by refusing air cover. This would crackle
the air waves, but later. Tall tales,
I figured, wrongly,
putting my fist in my glove
for America.
Moby Dick, you damn whale,
I've seen whales.
America, though—
too big to be seen.

Things I Took

The back shell of a crab.
Stones from the sea.
A feather and a duck's foot.
Too much thought about childhood.
Too many pictures
of my home town. The umbrella
the Union Avenue oaks made
down to the dock at the Bay.
The Little Dipper, easy to see.
The blown seeds of the dandelion,
the grass whistles,
the propellors weeds made,
the tests of flowers (love
and butter), the inks of berries.
And much more,
light as these things were.

Now they are back in place,
I can tell you
why I drove to Westhampton,
nearest the ocean,
the day of the hurricane.
From Bellport, I had seen the Atlantic
lapping Fire Island's
thinnest strip, where stilts
held up the houses while the dunes
moved inches for miles.
I hurried to cross a bridge
toward fury. That was my job.
Others were shuttering windows,
bringing in boats or just loosening
the ties and running. In 1938,
a storm brought some of Florida
to New York, and boats down Union,
trees down in the schoolyard
and enough mud and brine to pack a town in.

So much self!
Look at stanza one
compared to stanza two—the things
themselves, their specific
densities, differ. You can see
for yourself in what you remember
the place where strength of spirit
begins, the loss of words, etc.
For the soul doesn't call to itself,
nor is it locked in ice
when the water freezes, nor transported
by rushing water, unless the one
who watches watches by holding still.
In the wind, the soul is not always moving.
In the calm, the soul may not be.
Compare stanza one to stanza two.
Much more could have gone into the one,
nothing of consequence
into the other. I got as close
as I could before the waves
raked up enough of the ocean floor
to convince me.

The Canal at Rye

Don't let them tell you—
the women or the men—
they knew me.
You knew me.
Don't let them tell you
I didn't love your mother.
I loved her.
Or let them tell you.
Do you remember Rye?—
where the small fishing boats,
deprived of the receding sea,
took the tide out,
a canal so thin they had to go
single file, sails of suns,
while the red sun rose.
That town was old.
A great novelist lived there.
Do you know him?
Not many will be reading
his long sentences.
And they are punished.
For that is *our* sentence: to be
dumb in a passage we think turns
from darkness to light
but doesn't. Turn back
to art, including the sentence.
It is also the world. Whoever understands
the sentence understands
his or her life. There are reasons
not to, reasons too
to believe or not to. But
reasons do not complete an argument.
The natural end and extension
of language
is nonsense. Yet there is safety
only there. That is why Mr. Henry James
wrote that way—
out with the tide, but further.

The Last Thing I Say

to a thirteen-year-old sleeping,
tone of an angel, breath of a soft wing,
I say through an upright dark space
as I narrow it pulling the door
sleepily to let the words go surely into
the bedroom until I close them in
for good, a nightwatchman's-worth
of grace and a promise for morning
not so far from some God's first notion
that the world be an image by first light
so much better than pictures of hope
drawn by firelight in ashes,
so much clearer too, a young person
wanting to be a man might draw one finger
along an edge of this world and it
would slice a mouth there
to speak blood and then should he put that wound
into the mouth of his face,
he will be kissed there and taste
the salt of his father as he lowers
himself from his son's high bedroom
in the heaven of his image of
a small part of himself and sweet dreams.

Where Is Odysseus From and What Was He Before He Left for the Trojan War?

By a city building in Málaga—
upon a hill it was, but nothing important
had taken place or was taking place,
even inside us,
when we visited most of that year the five countries
in which the dollar was slipping
and fewer foreigners were tipping—
I found a pod that resembles
two shells of brown turtles,
hinged at one end, yawning at the other,
from which there escaped the tiniest wooden seeds
borne by the thinnest flakes of wings,
and no one there could say
what it was. So I took six.

On the brightest day, when I might have seen
a mermaid in the Mediterranean,
I saw the way the color changes
halfway out to the limits of particular vision.
It was green "here" and blue "out there."
It was sky-blue, where blue.
It was a put-up green, where green, a made
green, a vegetable green.

How could I know much?
I hadn't been there a year.
I had yet to say a single thing clearly
in the language.
I hadn't seen inside my shoulders
where they hurt for some reason.
I couldn't see behind me and go forward,
but I kept looking back.

It became a matter of a gummy substance
I scraped from a tree,
a matter of brittle y's of turtle-pods,
an importance of winged seeds,

an absolute blindness we see much of—
that takes the form most of all
of a love of nature.

No one has said this.

Five years later, I found again the turtle-pod
on a sub-tropical island,
and again no one could name it.
Again, I brought home three. Again,
I made a connection, I reached.

Yet
from every elsewhere,
we returned. From
the amazing propeller the guard wove
from a single weed
in sight of the gypsy caves of Granada.
From the fingers of broom,
the fields of mustard and gorse,
the England that hugs the hedges in Rye,
from the weight of stone that throws
itself into the water
at the far tip of Long Island
to best England,
and from far and away beyond our own language,
from Spain, from France, from Scotland,
and also from Morocco
that year.

It was our first trip abroad,
and we were thing-conscious. Oh, even to
Volubilis, Roman city raised
from the centuries
to be ruins. While a wind rose
that could lift a jacket from a chair back,

Where Is Odysseus From and What Was He Before He Left for the Trojan War?

and whitecaps moved north
to where Shelley stayed in 1812,
to where Wordsworth lived after he had lost it,
to where land begins and land ends.

It did not cease to be difficult.
The time it took to learn
from the many effects of travel
would be a long time,
like the time it takes a robin
in a dry spring full of enemies
to find and return with
a berry to soak and chew and then pass
from one mouth to another
in an instant.

We have not seen so much
that we may make of the woods a violin
to be played by the wind
while men must cure themselves.
Is there among us
one who can go anywhere
without looting or looking for ivory,
but advance the plot?

I renounce the souvenir,
the colorful photo, the clean stones and the pressed
leaves, the pods and the sponges.
I renounce the brass African sugar hammer
used by no one, the washed shells
emptied of life.

I shall keep the wide-bladed
pasta shears
because they made our supper
in Catalonia.

A Shrug

Let's see,
if I have it right,
the statue of Balzac that stands in Paris
resembling a tree, all feelingly
up from its roots (feet) like an *old* tree,
gnarled and corrugated—
this statue was damned because it looked too much
like a tree, all feelingly
up sexually, all outdoors-like, seemingly
open to anything,
maybe under his stone coat the great Balzac
is masturbating,
which gives his face the flush look
of its character
where the rain rains red
and the waiters push the young café crowd
out to linger in the rain for free.

You don't believe the rain is red?
Go and look.
Good dirt is always partly blue
and city rain is red.
It's a scandal that we continue
to speak of our water as clear
when we can see it in the air,
and to speak of our ideas
as inviolable ideals. The world can stuff our mouths
with the opaqueness of life
and violation.

I had a moment near Balzac in Paris
which I treasure.
A corner boy, one of those Left Bank schoolboys
who feed heavy jellied candies
to the coach class who empty mid-evenings
from the jittery budget hotels
on *Rue des Écoles*,
and from whom I bought something sticky,

palmed the better part of my change
and handed me the small bills only,
while he chattered like a host
of his great love for Americans.
This is a game I happen to know
to watch for when the talk turns Balzacian.
When I turned, he was ready
with my money, and a good smile in the silence.

Let's see,
if I have it right,
Rodin's *Balzac* was thought too rough, obscene,
and of course it was intended that way,
as if to keep something from you
until you want it,
and then to give it all to you with a shrug.

What's the matter?
You don't believe the rain in Paris is red?

What They Do to You in Distant Places

I never told you.
There was a woman—in the greening season
of a tropical island
where I had gone to break some hard thoughts
across my knee
and also, although I am no athlete
but breathe with my stomach like the satyr
and live in my stomach
according to bile and acid and bread and bitter chocolate,
to run a long race for the first time.
On that morning,
it was raining in great screens
of the purest water and almost no one at 4 a.m.
where I waited, half-sheltered
by the edge of my dark hotel, for a let-up.
Except her, suddenly
from nowhere—smelling of long hair and dew,
smelling of dew and grass and a little powder.
She wore a dress that moved.
She had been out dancing and the night and she
were young.
I wore a black watch cap like an old sailor
but I was all there was.

I said no, I had to do something else.
She asked how far? And
if I would run all that way—hours.
I said I'd try,
and then she kissed me for luck
and her mouth on mine was as sweet as the wild guava
and the smell of her hair
was that of the little bit of dew the lover
brings home from the park
when again she shows up in the morning.

I don't know where I have been
that I have ever had such a kiss
that asked nothing and gave everything.

I walked out into the rain
as if blessed. But I had forgotten
what they do to you in distant places,
taking away your memory
before sending you back. You and me.
I confess,
I forgot her within the hour
in the gross odors of my labors.
If I had known what she was doing. . . .
Perhaps she's with you now.

Italian

It would be enough
if Marvin, on his first scared journey
to Italy,
found there in the gassy rainbows
in puddles in the gear-stripped, tarred,
broken, bled on and often washed
streets of Rome
a sky to go home in. He must be
looking for something—
this child of an island—
to have crossed the ocean and Alps
without gold, without
one book on birds or plants. God,
how he hopes he hasn't come
just for a self-portrait.
So in the gassy air with green pears
and the arc of a banana
left from a pocket's lunch
leading him on. He has a habit of bananas
and of not peeling them in time.
They point at his feet and grow dark.
They are wasted.
But, if it comes to that,
they are not more wasted than marble,
which seems to have been used
to break the people's backs
and interrupt the sun
and find another use for sand.
The air there could make you remember
a drawling sea,
or corn gone ripe into colors
and gathered for the holidays. He won't
want to stay by himself.
He won't be satisfied to make tiny flowers of type
alone in the hotel or café.
He won't be made beautiful by the news
of our dancing. No,
he wants to know which word means really.

He wants to know which word tells where two streets meet,
which word means turning around fast.
He wants to know which word means not tied.
And which means frightening.
He needs to know which word means an outside covering
on a house, and which one means
you think something happened.
He wants to know how long the growing season is.
At home. Once he put a hand
into the water somewhere in a flat wintry light
and the whitefish were the bones of diamonds,
so why not anyone?

The Hedgeapple

I

I wish we'd gone back—
you didn't tell me she came off her porch
and ran through the green yards
waving us back as we drove away
but all the time in our blind spot.
That heavy fruit, the hedgeapple,
had made us stop. Then when she came waving
to the screen we flinched
a foot down on the gas pedal not to be
pinned for having intentions
on her hedgeapple tree.
She knew us,
she told you later,
but still we had the fear of correspondence,
and the guilt that comes from watching
someone else's treasure
in the open,
and also the fear of letting things be
more than they seem and ourselves less.
We should have gone back.

Do the trees really laugh?
Can we smell the light?
Is there smoke inside the cornstalk
and a light inside the tree,
a light that will not find where it came from?
What they call a hedgeapple—
it is one more perversion of the apple,
one more story like unto the ancient
unwilling airs and dances.
I am sure that we could have stolen one
and taken a bite apiece
and made ourselves crazy from the ground up.
We should have gone back.
We should have beckoned the wind
back into the hedgeapples
and her back in through the screen.

2

In spring, when the trees laugh,
like men and women who have been breathing
deeply and are also thirsty,
and the light
increases and increases
its waxy luxury so that a stand of bush
might seem an artist's wash,
we forget
what we were told.

First, the hedgeapple
is the giant birthing of a tree,
not a hedge, and second,
is no apple. A lemon grapefruit, maybe.
Like a grapefruit, but green.
Like an apple, but lemony.

We were lucky,
three in a car, the language we spoke
seeming to make light everywhere
because we stopped to look.
For a moment then, we forgot
what we were told.
And we didn't think.
Without us, the hedgeapple is perfect—
means nothing.
We should have gone back.
I am sure now she was watching us
from the beginning,
and the whole time too.

We thought we didn't take her hedgeapple.
We should have given it back.

So: here.

Drawn by Stones, by Earth,
by Things that Have Been
in the Fire

(1 9 8 4)

Drawn by Stones, by Earth, by Things that Have Been in the Fire

I can tell you about this because I have held in my hand
the little potter's sponge called an "elephant ear."
Naturally, it's only a tiny version of an ear,
but it's the thing you want to pick up out of the toolbox
when you wander into the deserted ceramics shop
down the street from the cave where the fortune-teller works.
Drawn by stones, by earth, by things that have been in the fire.

The elephant ear listens to the side of the vase
as it is pulled upwards from a dome of muddy clay.
The ear listens to the outside wall of the pot
and the hand listens to the inside wall of the pot,
and between them a city rises out of dirt and water.
Inside this city live the remains of animals,
animals who prepared for two hundred years to be clay.

Rodents make clay, and men wearing spectacles make clay,
though the papers they were signing go up in flames
and nothing more is known of these long documents
except by those angels who divine in our ashes.
Kings and queens of the jungle make clay
and royalty and politicians make clay although
their innocence stays with their clothes until unravelled.

There is a lost soldier in every ceramic bowl.
The face on the dinner plate breaks when the dish does
and lies for centuries unassembled in the soil.
These things that have the right substance to begin with,
put into the fire at temperatures that melt glass,
keep their fingerprints forever, it is said,
like inky sponges that walk away in the deep water.

The White Pony

1

Where is the book in which I wished to look again?
There on page two hundred and seventy-seven,
a poet of indescribable lightness,
a poet who could speak with birds and trees,
likened herself to a flower—revealing
only that the flower was yellow,
revealing neither its name nor location,
nor the depth and length of its knowledge.
Since, I have been everywhere in search of it.
Not in books only, but deep in alleys and woods,
where I see that I am neither tree nor city
weed, growing in concrete, nor any flower.
Perhaps if I could choose for myself a color,
I might become like all objects given that color,
and I myself might impart my color
to each dimension, and in all directions.
I shall be white, the white of all colors at once,
the white behind yellow, beneath the sky,
at the edge of an eye, or a fingernail or toenail,
the white where no letters appear on the page,
the white that surrounds the voice that says,
"I am thinner than a yellow flower."

2
And now I find it again. Loafing
in the bath, I see that on this page
the flower is named by a conscientious editor.
A chrysanthemum. Favorite of a friend.
I find that I am not pleased to be informed.
It is as though I could see in the air about me
a road for the wind, or in the forest
a hook to pull the trees up to their full height.
I did not wish to know so much.
Let her be just a chrysanthemum for the knowing.
I believe she is also the slenderness of yellow,
and moves like a curtain at an open window
and speaks with the owl in the daytime.
I believe she could not have written one such line
and lived as I see some others of my time living—
so big and proud they are, and keep records.
She who is the yellow of a flower in the sun
must touch the white wastes, the accumulations.
And she is thin, who can bow low.

Trees as Standing for Something

1

More and more it seems I am happy with trees
and the light touch of exhausted morning.
I wake happy with her soft breath on my neck.
I wake happy but I am happier yet.
For my loves are like the leaves in summer.
But oh!, when they fall, and I wake with a start,
will I feel the sting of betrayal and ask, What is this
love, if it has to end, even in death,
or if one might lose it even during a life?
Who will care for such a thing?
Better to cut it down where it stands.
Better to burn it, and to burn with it,
than to turn around to see one's favorite gone.

2

It began when they cut down the elm and I let them.
When the corkscrew willow withered and I said nothing.
Then when the soft maple began to blow apart,
when the apple tree succumbed to poison,
the pine to a matrix of bugs, the oak to age,
it was my own limbs that were torn off, or so it seemed,
and my love, which had lived through many storms,
died, again and again. Again and again, it perished.
What was I to say then but Oh, Oh, Oh, Oh, Oh!
Now you see a man at peace, happy and happier yet,
with her breath on the back of his neck in the morning,
and of course you assume it must always have been this way.
But what was I to say, then and now, but Oh! and Oh! Oh!

Leaving a Resort Town

Get away, said something that wasn't
human, and I took a fix on distance.
Sometimes when I see what became
of those breakers—low and thin now
in the parking lot, or soggy underfoot
where the yard slants toward the creek—
and the wind—sometimes you have to
watch the trees to see it—
I know what spoke.

At home, here, they say
sink, sink, not that other thing;
and *listen, listen*, not what others said.
Any sea is a farm, and you can hum
and walk until, far, you hear yourself
again. Land: no edge, no end.
Suppose you always got where you were going.

Who & Where

I

Where I live, it's a long uphill to
the Great Divide where larger men crossed
a streak in the land rivers know.
Somewhere else there may be gold in the trees
or dollars in the view. Here, we may be
nowhere ourselves but everywhere
on the way—so stop sometimes. We've eats,
nights, scars on the land, earth

you can pick up and squeeze,
the obvious. Sometimes we leave in
a line of dirt in a crack of skin.
If you drive past, you may see strange creatures
crossing the land, leaving behind them
heaps, bales, piles, clumps. And in the land:
supply lines, lost fingers, implements
left to rust where nothing now will grow.

2
Who I am is a short person with small feet
and fingers. When the hill is snowy,
I have to walk on the grass, and this gives
me a different viewpoint and wet shoes.
I see writers grow huge
in their writings. I get smaller yet,
so small that sometimes a tree is more
than I can look up to. I am down here with
all the other tiny, weak things. Sure,
once in a while I pull myself up
to assert something to the air, but oftener
I look for what was lost in the weeds.
The Gods drink nectar, I drink fruit juice.
All my life, people have told me,
"You are big, or will be." But I'm small.
I am not at the center of the circle.
I am not part of the ring. Like you,
I am not the core, the dark star or the lit star.
I take a step. The wind takes a step.
I take a drink of water. The earth swallows.
I just live here—like you, like you, like you.

Felt but Not Touched

That light behind the Olympics at supper hour—
it takes a sky of clouds from here to there
to spot the sun, seam and snow just right.
That pulsating light, a sizable incandescence
out of the grayness—that's the wing or tail of a plane.
The roundness of things—that's knowledge, a new way
to touch it here. (On the plains, we see Earth curve,
and I have seen the sun melt into the ocean elsewhere
and then call a color or two it left behind down.)

Then it is dark. The great streak of sunlight
that showed our side of snowy peaks has gone ahead.
Those bumps on the holly tree we passed
getting home for the late afternoon view from upstairs—
next to them, some smaller trees and a porch,
and next to that the streaky windows and then
the whole household getting ready to make the break
into spring—and sometimes in late winter we can't
sit still for connecting time at both ends.

If anything we do or don't will keep the world
for others, it will need such distant knowledge—beyond
experience, provable by ones, felt but not touched.
As we watch the light in the distance move on and around,
and the air at mountain height take up the cause of snow,
all that is beneath us that is not light has stopped.

Against Stuff

What is it that I should be
to be able to look out at night beyond
whatever intrudes
and see there, undistracted by sunlight
on the hard edges of machines
or shining out from the glassy eyeballs
of men and women going to work,—
see there what I need, or you need, or god
forbid the world
will have been said to have needed
if anyone survives
the coming instantaneous flaming
of all books and other records, people
and animals and vegetation
and machines which could not suffer
that much light at one time?

I do not believe for a moment that the last
poet in the last standing building
while the world splits up and caves inward
like the crust of a rich cake
will be trying to make a line come out right;
nor does it seem remotely possible
to anyone who believes, as I do,
that those standards and agreements
which will have brought us
our end, as well as any last
prospecting of the future, any last words,
could possibly be right;
and, if we are shortly to find ourselves
without beast, field or flower,
is it not right that we now prepare
by removing them from our poetry?

The beauty that goes up in flame
is touchable beauty—the beauty of things
in light; of all manner of representing
people, mouths open or closed forever;

and of beauty known by its shape
in the dark, or by whatever hides and reveals it—
beauty received, registered,
the object of study, talent and abandon.
But still there is another beauty
known to us by such measures as "yesterday,"
"tomorrow," "at a distance," or
"inextricable and transcendent," and which
we cannot be, but can only conceive
and cause. Will we, always?
I suggest, knowing that every form and habit
has been described, that the forms are wrong,

the habits harmful, and the objects too many.
If I can see, it is only because it is dark.

Questions to Answers

For my unique voice,
for my solitary vision,
I was given the song of a bird
outside my window
and all of the songs that answered
to it.
For my way with words,
for my unusual behavior, listen,
I was given an essence of chocolate
which only made me desire
all other chocolates.
For my individual grief,
for my perfect isolation,
I was given maps to mass graves
on every continent
and still for my feet I was given shoes
and for my hands gloves in winter
and now if I ask
whose shoes otherwise and whose
gloves if not mine
I offend those who liked my poems
for a while.
And this is why I have come to believe
that there are, to my questions,
answers
after all.

Jane Was with Me

Jane was with me
the day the rain dropped a squirrel *like that*.
An upside-down embrace,
a conical explosion from the sky,
a thick flowering of sudden water—
whatever it was,
the way it happened is
that first the trees grew a little,
and then they played music
and breathed songs and applauded themselves,
and that made the squirrel
surrender to nothing but the beauty
of a wet tree
about to shake its upper body like the devil.
And of course, of course,
he went out on that tree just as far as he could
when things were not so beautiful
and that was it: hard onto the roof of our car
before he could set his toes.

The flat whack of the body.
He lay in the street breathing and bleeding
until I could get back,
and then he looked me in the eye exactly.
Pasted to the concrete by his guts,
he couldn't lift, or leave, or live.
And so I brought the car and put its right tire
across his head. If in between
the life part and the death part,
there is another part,
a time of near-death,
we have come to know its length and its look
exactly—in this life always near death.
But there's something else.
Jane was with me.
After the rain, the trees were prettier yet.
And if I were a small animal with a wide tail,
I would trust them too. Especially
if Jane were with me.

White Clover

Once when the moon was out about three-quarters
and the fireflies who are the stars
of backyards
were out about three-quarters
and about three-fourths of all the lights
in the neighborhood
were on because people can be at home,
I took a not so innocent walk
out among the lawns,
navigating by the light of lights,
and there there were many hundreds of moons
on the lawns
where before there was only polite grass.
These were moons on long stems,
their long stems giving their greenness
to the center of each flower
and the light giving its whiteness to the tops
of the petals. I could say
it was light from stars
touched the tops of flowers and no doubt
something heavenly reaches what grows outdoors
and the heads of men who go hatless,
but I like to think we have a world
right here, and a life
that isn't death. So I don't say it's better
to be right here. I say this is where
many hundreds of core-green moons
gigantic to my eye
rose because men and women had sown green grass,
and flowered to my eye in man-made light,
and to some would be as fire in the body
and to others a light in the mind
over all their property.

Three Letters

Dear ——————,

I am green, and I may well misunderstand your words, as even now I cannot read the precise condensations of rain upon the outside of the thick glass of a recessed window on the fourth floor where I write this. Through the gray slats of window blinds, they line up like hieroglyphics, and I am as certain that I do not think correctly about this as I am that they should always appear to me to be amorphous cartoons squeezed from the weather unless I take steps. . . .

And so I might crack my fist against the glass, not changing a line of that watery writing which maintains its distance and temperature, but, in the pain and insanity with which I think of my battered hand, comes to be, in a life which has sides, the other side.

I detest the way that life is used as a metaphor for death, which only gives us death as a metaphor for life. I would rather have this sense of the other side, the condensed version, the utterly unreachable. For if I break through this window to take possession of what is on its other side, what will be left?

Only everything.

Dear ——————,

Today, when I pulled on a rope to open the blinds, the day was bright with light clouds like those which surround the peaks of the world's tallest mountains. And now the air is moving around enough to bend the tops of trees. An altogether satisfactory amalgam of wishes as portrayed in pictures and talk.

Behind a choppy cluster of full trees which ends my view in one direction within a hundred yards, there sits a small chapel rarely used now. Almost no one married in it is still married. It's not cursed. It is just very ordinary.

Others are bigger or smaller and known for it.

The chapel is open today. A ceremony for a woman who died in Ireland, who once wore her hair long enough to touch the floor when she bowed, and who danced in circles of head and hair until the force of it flung her from this town and out of mind.

No doubt she thought she was a failure. Most businessmen and scientists and everyone in the arts think they are. I think she intended to live longer. As I do. I know more and more people who are dead, which doesn't make them live. And I won't tell you how to say the end of that sentence. The mind can make all sounds at once.

The mind, starting from nothing but the privilege of darkness . . .

The mind, pulp and sinew, is destined never to complete a thought. As a life is destined to stop short, even if you live to be a hundred. In deception and pride, we have manufactured things to call complete. We are ourselves pieces of something, I am sure, but it would take the thinking of light itself to know what.

You wanted only to know how the river runs here, where the swords are among the trees, why the yellow flower is heading for the clouds, and maybe the attitude of the grass where some of the mourners are walking slowly towards the chapel, hands hanging heavily, rolling their steps so as to walk even more quietly. And I, I wanted to think about how time stops.

They are all in the chapel now, and the door closed.

Dear —————,

Your very friendliness is a problem when we come to speak about feelings, so that sometimes we hurry into lovemaking so that we might not suffer any longer the slight feeling of mere happiness.

We want someone to be watching when we do these things that might kill us. We can only see ourselves in the other's face. Not in the eyes only but in the mouth and cheeks. Is the mouth held open and sounds pushed up from stomach and bowels held caught at the top of the throat? Then someone must be reaching deeper to grab and pull out those sounds. Does the mouth contort and the teeth come forward? Then great labors are taking place to open up the body. Do the eyes slam shut? Then you and she are nothing, a long explosion seen and heard by no one, a triumph without beauty or ugliness, in which the smallest grain of feeling punctures the skin like one of those jacketed bullets which penetrates an armored vehicle of war and slams about inside, chewing up metal and skin until it stops spinning and drops.

Later, a door or hatch may open and a soldier appear seemingly undamaged and fall out as if unable to work his legs. Right now, it appears that no one has been left alive.

A True Story

One afternoon in my room
in Rome,
I found, wedged
next to the wheel of a wardrobe,
so far under
no maid's broom could touch it,
a pouch made from a sock.
Inside were diamonds
in several sizes. Spread on the carpet,
they caught in my throat.
I knew that, from that moment on,
I would never answer the door.
All of my holiday
would be a preparation
for leaving. First,
I would have to leave the hotel,
probably the city.
I knew someone I could trust
and another with nerve.
She would carry home
half of them, perhaps in her underwear,
if it was not of the kind
customs officers like to touch.
I would carry the others
by way of Zurich,
stopping to purchase
eucalyptus cigarettes, chocolates
and a modest music box
with its insides exposed.
After that, who knows?
Keep them for years?
Lug them into the shade and sell cheap?
A trip to a third country?
A middleman?

So long as I didn't look up,
there with the stones before me
in the old room in the old city—

where embellishment of every fixture
and centuries of detail
took precedence
over every consideration
of light, air or space—
so long as I did not look up
to my suspicion,
I held the endless light of a fortune
and the course of a lifetime.

In retrospect, it was entirely appropriate
that my diamonds
were the ordinary pieces
of a chandelier, one string of which
had been pulled down
by a previous tenant of room three,
perhaps in a fit of ecstacy.
For I found, also—a diamond-
shaped third of its cover
hanging down from behind the wardrobe,
face to the wall—
the current issue of one of those men's
monthlies in which half-
nude women, glossy with wealth,
ooze to escape
from their lingerie.
And in the single page in its center,
someone had held his favorite
long enough to make love.
The pages were stuck together elsewhere also,
in no pattern,
and the articles on clothing and manners
left untouched.

So this was no ordinary hotel room,
or the most ordinary of all!
Men had come here many times no doubt
to make love by themselves.

But now
it was also a place of hidden treasure.
The rush of wealth and dark promise
I took from that room
I also put back. And so too everyone
who, when in Rome,
will do what the Romans do.

They

My destiny has been to prune one tree
to make it look more and more common.
Friends, I am still at it.

It has been suggested
that I permit myself to be tattooed all over
and become, myself, a tree. Stick my arms out.

But that wouldn't be me. Nor would there be,
afterwards, as there is now,
the object of my desire

in the form of my desire unveiling.
What do they think this is all about?
Nothing was known before I came to know it.

The purpose of a tree is that I have given it:
to be the sane result of chaos,
to be so completely known it may be overlooked.

Two Implements

Sugar Hammer

It is not necessary to describe such things as a sugar hammer. It is enough to realize that the sweetest things in the world, from the lowliest crystals aspiring to be rock candy up to the entire substance of an intimate group of ladies and gentlemen chatting on the highly varnished deck of a pleasure boat as it takes them from A to B, summed up in the shimmering river and the sherry in their glasses, are not here for us to sample without battering, wrenching and the daily exhaustion of half our gain in the effort itself. Throwaways—poisoned, broken, inaccessible, unknown secrets of worms and mold. Hence, the sugar hammer is half cleaver.

Pasta Shears

Wide-bladed pasta shears, you would make a miserable job of a haircut and fail utterly at trousers or paper dolls. Like all scissors, you talk talk talk and eat eat eat. Someone must be cooking a lot of spaghetti! But forgive me if I poke fun. I have seen the famous rivers of Rome and Paris where one finds on the banks in the mornings the soggy remains of love and the emptied vessels of spirits. Things severed there—a sudden loss of feeling after the explosion of romance, or the onset of a chill when the liquor has run out—will never again be whole. What silent rite is practiced by those who wield scissors? It might not do to know. For if pasta could speak . . . , or beans . . . , or cloth or paper . . . , or those animals who make such a racket in the slaughterhouses . . . , or men and women who have so many objects of use and so many uses for each . . . .

Instructions to Be Left Behind

I've included this letter in the group
to be put into the cigar box—the one
with the rubber band around it you will find
sometime later. I thought you might
like to have an example of the way in which
some writing works. I may not say anything
very important or phrase things just-so,
but I think you will pay attention anyway
because it matters to you—I'm sure it does,
no one was ever more loved than I was.

What I'm saying is, your deep attention
made things matter—made art,
made science and business
raised to the power of goodness, and sport
likewise raised a level beyond.
I am not attaching to this a photograph
though no doubt you have in your mind's eye
a clear image of me in several expressions
and at several ages all at once—which is
the great work of imagery beyond the merely
illustrative. Should I stop here for a moment?

These markings, transliterations though they are
from prints of fingers, and they from heart
and throat and corridors the mind guards,
are making up again in you the one me
that otherwise would not survive that manyness
daisies proclaim and the rain sings much of.
Because I love you, I can almost imagine
the eye for detail with which you remember
my face in places indoors and out and far-flung,
and you have only to look upwards to see
in the plainest cloud the clearest lines
and in the flattest field your green instructions.

Shall I rest a moment in green instructions?
Writing is all and everything, when you care.
The kind of writing that grabs your lapels
and shakes you—that's for when you don't care
or even pay attention. This isn't that kind.
While you are paying your close kind of attention,
I might be writing the sort of thing you think
will last—as it is happening, now, for you.
While I was here to want this, I wanted it,
and now that I am your wanting me to be myself
again, I think myself right up into being
all that you (and I too) wanted me to be: You.

One of the Animals

Why does a dog get sick?
—You tell me.

What does he do about it?
—You tell me.

Does it make a difference?
—You tell me.

Does he live or die?
—You tell me.

Does it make a difference?
—That one I know.

Does it prepare you?
—That one I know too.

Will we know what to do?
—You tell me.

The Stones

One night in my room
many stones brought together over the years,
each bearing the gouges and pinpricks
of sea and shore life,
and each weighted according to the sea
which first chisels a slate
and then washes it and later writes on it
with an eraser—
these stones, large and small, flat,
rounded, conical, shapely or rough-hewn,
discussed their origins,
and then got around to me. One of them,
the white one full of holes
that wipes off on your hands, said
that he thinks I carry much sadness,
the weight of a heart full of stones,
and that I bring back these others
so that I might live among the obvious
heaviness of the world.
But another said that I carried him
six months in Spain
in a pants pocket and lifted him out
each night to place on the dresser,
and although he is small and flat,
like a planet seen from the moon,
I often held him up to the light,
and this is because I am able to lift
the earth itself. And isn't this
happiness? But a third stone spoke
from where it stood atop papers
and accused me of trying to manage
the entire world, which for the most part
is neither myself nor not myself,
and is also the air around the rim
of a moving wheel, the space beyond Space,
the water within water,
and the weight within the stone.
Then they all asked what right had I

to be happy or unhappy,
when the language of stones
was no different
from the language of a white lump of dung
among the excellent vegetables.

Banyan Tree Before the Civic Center, Honolulu

Hairy
like a man wearing a dress.
You don't speak with me the way the others
do, who tell me,
by green effort, by every half-drowning
and abdomen-push of new leaf,
they want to be trees,
trees tall enough to see over the trees.

You'll stay here and spread out, you say,
in a rumble of a voice
muffled by hair.
You are growing all up out of yourself!

Your roots are branches
so your leaves are the lawn!

If that's the way you are going to be—
deluxe, warm, a sexual fence
with the shapeliness of so many—
then you may have to become an entire nation
yourself,
just yourself in the center and also at the edges.

Who will want anything to do with you?
You get all over us.
You are an old man at heart.

I pity you,
freak among nations made up of individuals,
for you are an individual
composed of multitudes.

When a man wears a dress
or has so many legs,
it will always be noticed,
unless he is trying to pass for a tree.

Youth

Begins again in a kiss, in a passionate word,
begins where lazy fingers again feel suddenly
the surface of an ordinary thing—
in a gesture larger than anything a person can say,
and all this in a moment smaller than a second,
in a look that passes, in the flicker of a star,
as in between two ratchetings of a turning wheel.

How fat the English sparrows had become!
How limp the lovebirds seemed in their slow movements!
They say that, in winter, ice will warm the water
beneath it, but people will tell you anything.
There are people anxious to tell you you are losing
your hair, your mind, your slender disposition
and good luck, failing to live up to a promise

you never made. I remember the look of the fields
the day I came flying home from beautiful Elsewhere
to the racks of sunstruck corn suffering summer.
How beautiful were these rediscovered rectangles
beneath our wings, down there dumb to intention
in the black truth of an indifferent earth.
I had been away, and darkly thought again of you.

Unless It Was Courage

Again today, balloons aloft in the hazy *here*,
three heated, airy, basket-toting balloons,
three triangular boasts ahead against the haze
of summer and the gravity of onrushing fall—
these win me from the wavery *chrr*-ing of locusts
that fills these days the air between the trees,
from the three trembly outspreading cocoons hanging
on an oak so old it might have been weighed down
by the very thought of hundreds of new butterflies,
and from all other things that come in threes
or seem to be arranged. These *are* arranged,
they are the perfection of mathematics as idea,
they have lifted off by making the air greater—
nothing else was needed unless it was courage—
and today they do not even drag a shadow.

It was only a week ago I ran beneath one.
All month overhead had passed the jetliners,
the decorated company planes, the prop jobs
and great crows of greed and damage (I saw one
dangle a white snake from its bill as it flew),
and all month I had looked up from everywhere
to see what must seem from other galaxies
the flies of heaven. Then quickly my chance came,
and I ran foolish on the grass with my neck bent
to see straight up into the great resonant cavity
of one grandly wafting, rising, bulbous, whole
balloon, just to see nothing for myself. That
was enough, it seemed, as it ran skyward and away.
There I was, unable to say what I'd seen.
But I was happy, and my happiness made others happy.

Personal Reasons

Your hair—short, long; stars, a bed
under stars, moon; your stars, your moon,
your embrace, your circumstances, my
buttons, your earrings; your collections
of moonlight in darkened rooms—let it all
fall when it will: so surrounded are we
already by all that we have lost
to each other, we could be god and goddess,
we could be grass and sky, flower and tree,
two of anything in romantic proximity. But
we are—that's it—one man and one woman,
alike we choose to believe. But it
(you and me) wasn't always that way,
or not so very much that very way—us.

In

In the earth, where there are stones, dimes, fingers.
In dirt, where there is soul and spirit.

In rain, in steps.
In sand, in fields of insects.

In fields of insects.
In victory-tailed swallows—

in the furious company of swallows where I walk
in the field, stirring insects, bargaining

in swallow-talk for company.
In victory-tailed swallow-talk as they eat.

In 1983. In Port Townsend, Wa.
In a mood to find the one tree, magic stone, pirate coin.

In the dark morning on wet sand with the gulls.
In the bright sky toward which we look to see

in death certain people we know who are gone.
In Dick Hugo, a child who wrote the poetry of a grownup.

In saying no more about it.
In asking neither praise nor blame in the name of mortality.

In living right here, where we find ourselves,
in who we are right now.

In who we are right now among the swallows eating insects
in a field, in pain from wanting too much.

In shade, then shadow. In life. In concert.
In the sign the swallows flash as they win the day.

Days of Time

1 *To Be*

How could I wake from childhood
when everywhere I went there was breathing
like a mother's breath at the ear of her child
before words; when in all places
there was touch and people who defied
the magazines, who did not look perfect and dead;
when my bodyguard was luck
and my texts were songs and the humming of the planets.

It was necessary that I hear a sizzle
in the lungs, and a hum on the wires. Fate decreed
that the magazines should multiply,
the child in me gradually decipher the air,
and the planets die. Fate, which is Kingdom Come,
called me out of the crowd
where I was shopping or doing some busywork,
and told me to stop singing and just be.

But I had an idea. Didn't the sun make it impossible
to look at the sun? Wasn't the night
known only by nuance, the darkness unstudied?
If I contained the earth and all of its flowers
but did not once look at them, would anyone know?
Thus, in my neighborhood, passion—even rapture!—
survived in secret, and still a child appears
in the guise of a grownup at dusk and story-time.

2   *In Those Days*

In those days, I was pulled as if by an undertow
from a far sea, and beauty; and hastening, fastening
my buttons as I went, I hurried to reach the delta
before a single wing took flight, and constantly
I was the black-robed trumpeter attending dawn,
playing into the brassy announcements of the sun
my Hindemith, my Haydn, my melancholy Voluntary.
And I was Taps and the muted echo of Taps.

All of this required a youthful half-stupor
through which I could make out many stone valleys
connected by corridors and windows. At each window:
voices without sound, a hook for my red jacket,
and a dreamy scene in the rain where back porches
were lit by candles. Phosphor in the paint on the ceiling
gave constellations their shine where they turned.
In reality, it was I who was turning; it was I at the window.

How did we find our way from the forced beginning
of each school day to the final bell? The daily miracle!
Someday, the bills will come due for the things we did
to save our souls—this much for writing on the walls,
for carving our names in the desks, this much
for a bad mouth, this much for sleeping in class. . . .
Something glazed our eyes and held our attention—
some mortar in the bloodstream, some blood in the cement.

3   *The Facts of Life*

This pebble never thought it would surface here
where I came walking to scuff it, wreck it, bother it,
and utterly transform it from a simple creature
of limited experience in the darkness of its mother
into a highly valued, polished star of daylight.
I, of course, was just passing the time by rolling it
back and forth under the sole of my shoe.

A psychiatrist would say I was worried at the time,
but I would say I was worried *all* of the time—
here with the trees taking sick and even the healthiest
rocking in the dirt from this disaster and that one,
so that bare plots of land where prairie grass shone
took up with tumult and history, forever locked,
and rocks appeared on cleared land without warning.

It's as if something in nature were asking my help,
but modestly, reluctantly, as politely as a black shoe.
I stood where I might see what was asked for,
by the dry sites of immense basements for new buildings
where pipe was being laid in the dusty man-made rivers
which run down everywhere beneath the deepest roots.
I stood and worked my foot back and forth like a rolling pin.

Out of the throat of the world, a pebble emerged.
And it said nothing, or was muffled before it could speak
by the innocence of bystanders, by the facts of life.
Dingy and shipwrecked, the buildings rose higher.
When the men broke from work under the threat of rain,
I took that star of daylight, my little marble,
into my hand, where it helped me to cut my way home.

4   *Days of Time*

Gone into the woods, they'll say, only because
I preferred the company of trees, any kind of tree,
to the company of . . . . It was a day like this one,
in the dark season, a time when one sits in the center
avoiding the flat wind that blows through the walls,
that time when icy vapors hover above the river
and the big pines move like old men in dark clothes
for an important occasion: the days of time, time of time.

Gone into the sea, they'll say, just because
I loved to walk on the darkened sand at the weed line
near to the scalloped edge of the ocean, and there
felt on the soles of my feet as the spent waves receded
the termites of ocean floors and the crab imprint
that gives the galaxy a picture of the galaxy.
It was a wide day in the sunshine, but narrow in the shadows,
when I walked around a bend in the beach and stayed.

Disappeared into thin air, they'll say, because
I stopped to look up at a giant red fan in the clouds
and a picture of four bakers peeking over the horizon,
and counted the wooden thread-spools in a cigar box.
It was a day like this one: sulphur hung in the air,
somewhere the earth vented the steam at its core.
It was a day in the future, just like this in the future,
when the melting wax no longer seemed to betray the candle.

Starfish

His entire body is but one hand, severed at the wrist. It lies on the sand in the late afternoon as if sunning itself. As he dries, he reaches ever more arthritically for the light itself with which to brown his palm. In this regard, his futility is unsurpassed.

You may pick him up now. Dead hand in your live hand. The mount of flesh just behind the thumb has been planed down and the soft tissue, tissue that will never tan, seems to have endured much scraping and dragging on the roughest edges of the sea, and to have fought back by raising its hackles, as it were, until it has become a hand of tiny spikes, but spikes nonetheless. Rub him in your palm, if you like. His hand is tougher than your own.

Of course, this starfish that we know is only the version run aground, becalmed, out of its element, preserved, petrified. In its lifetime, which we have missed entirely, it was soft, it was spongy, it was bread to the sea. Then, it molded itself to its element, water, not as a hand closes around a prized possession to become a fist, but as a wheel becomes motion without losing its shape even for a moment.

The starfish, alive, was a kind of wheel. The sea was its air, as all around us in what we call a universe are stars in space like fish in the ocean. Like fish, we know them only at a distance, we approach closer to them by means of glass and mirrors, we grow silent in the presence of the mysterious nature of them, we may only imagine touching them when they have been cast up on the beach or thrown down from light.

Such is our conception of Heaven, from which it seems we are forever finding souvenirs, signals, clues. We have no way of knowing whether, at any single moment, we are being led toward a Heaven that follows upon our lives or toward one that precedes it, or indeed whether or not these may be the same. Is it not then natural that we look down in the light and up in the darkness, and is it not also ironic that it requires a dark, absorbent object to stop our gaze in the former while it takes a moment of hard light to focus us in the latter? We shall never know the end of our thoughts, nor where they began.

Return to our starfish now. Time has given it a new, earthy odor.

The Nest

The day the birds were lifted from my shoulders,
the whole sky was blue, a long-imagined effect
had taken hold, and a small passenger plane
was beating the earth with its wings
as it swung over the bean fields toward home.
A fat car barely travelled a narrow road
while I waited at the bottom of a hill.
People around me were speaking loudly
but I heard only whispers, and stepped away.

You understand, I was given no choice.
For a long time, I was tired of whatever it was
that dug its way into my shoulders for balance
and whispered in my ears, and hung on for dear life
among tall narrow spaces in the woods
and in thickets and crowds, like those of success,
with whom one mingles at parties and in lecture halls.
In the beginning, there was this or that . . .
but always on my shoulders that which had landed.

That was life, and it went on in galleries
and shopping plazas, in museums and civic centers,
much like the life of any responsible man
schooled in the marriage of history and culture
and left to learn the rest at the legs of women.
In furtive rooms, in passing moments, the sea
reopened a door at its depth, trees spoke
from the wooden sides of houses, bodies became
again the nests in the naked tree.

After that, I was another person,
without knowing why or how, and after that,
I lived naked in a new world where the sun
broke through windows to grasp entire families
and crept between trees to wash down streets
without disturbing any object, in a world
where a solitary kiss blew down a door.
The day the birds were lifted from my shoulders,
it killed me—and almost cost me a life. . . .

New Poems

Wednesday

Gray rainwater lay on the grass in the late afternoon.
The carp lay on the bottom, resting, while dusk took shape
in the form of the first stirrings of his hunger,
and the trees, shorter and heavier, breathed heavily upwards.
Into this sodden, nourishing afternoon I emerged,
partway toward a paycheck, halfway toward the weekend,
carrying the last mail and holding above still puddles
the books of noble ideas. Through the fervent branches,
carried by momentary breezes of local origin,
the palpable Sublime flickered as motes on broad leaves,
while the Higher Good and the Greater Good contended
as sap on the bark of the maples, and even I
was enabled to witness the truly Existential where it loitered
famously in the shadows as if waiting for the moon.
All this I saw in the late afternoon in the company of no one.

And of course I went back to work the next morning. Like you,
like anyone, like the rumored angels of high office,
like the demon foremen, the bedeviled janitors, like you,
I returned to my job—but now there was a match-head in my thoughts.
In its light, the morning increasingly flamed through the window
and, lit by nothing but mind-light, I saw that the horizon
was an idea of the eye, gilded from within, and the sun
the fiery consolation of our nighttimes, coming far.
Within this expectant air, which had waited the night indoors,
carried by—who knows?—the rhythmic jarring of brain tissue
by footsteps, by colors visible to closed eyes, by a music
in my head, knowledge gathered that could not last the day,
love and error were shaken as if by the eye of a storm,
and it would not be until quitting that such a man
might drop his arms, that he had held up all day since the dew.

Replica

The fake Parthenon in Nashville, Stonehenge reduced by a quarter
near Maryhill on the Columbia, the little Statue of Liberty
taken from the lawn of the high school and not recovered for months,
Sam Roditi's Watts Towers in the tilemaker's shape of a ship
to sail home in, the house in the shape of a ship near Milwaukee
where once before the river below rose up to swallow the bank,
World's Fairs where one can enter the cell of a human body
or see Paris, London, Marrakesh and the Taj Mahal in one afternoon,
the headache that may be sinus or bad eyes or allergy or a tumor,
the bruise that was blue now yellow the effect of labor or abuse,
the cataclysmic event in a personal life now totally forgotten,
the memory of doing well that turned to unexpressed anger
just because love was everywhere preventing helpless mistakes—
achievement and perfection for the first time considered in error,
the end of life being life itself, life itself ignorance,
we never tire of making the world smaller, looking in dollhouses,
and a mailman who has picked up every bright piece of glass and tile
in forty years of rounds retires to build a house of glass and tile
which is his life, no kick coming, while in a suburb of Chicago
a leaning tower of Pisa drawn to scale signals a shopping plaza
where goods come in from around the world, for the people who live
     there.
And Vico says gods and goddesses are the self writ large—
selves to make earthquakes, tornados, eclipses, selves to lift the sun—
and Vico says all things having been named for the namers, us,
we give a chair arms, legs, a seat and a back, a cup has its lip
and a bottle its neck, and ever after rivers flow from their headwaters
and a well-oiled engine purrs at the center of good feeling.
So take your misery down a notch in aches and pains and little diseases,
in years of photo albums, in journals of dreams interrupted by
     mornings,
in furniture you built yourself, in copies and imitations,
in scale model wars and families and the age of fancy automobiles.
And when once in your life you make the big trip to the original,
chances are you'll mainly see your own face in the glass that protects
everything of which there's one only in the form of its only maker.

The Politics of an Object

The banana is stronger than the human head in the following ways: those fine threads that wave from the top knot are harder to break than hair. Should you pick one up, you cannot resist peeling it: it will have done to it what it was born to have done to it. As for endurance and sacrifice: while thousands of well-muscled laborers did not survive the cheap labor of imperialism in their republics, and others died with their mouths stuffed full of money, the banana hung on, gathering potassium. It knew the future, it knew its history, it was prepared for bruises. I have gathered the small colorful stickers applied one to a bunch until now they cover the wooden arms of the chair where I often linger in the kitchen to chat with my wife. The bananas don't last long, eaten or not. But each of the tiny stickers, each company logo, stays in place incorruptibly, and, though I am but one man, without a plan, I am keeping their names in mind. So you see? A banana is superior to a human head because it gives up without a fight. And still there is a future.

The Pill

The pill, in the pill bottle, humming like a wheel at rest, confident that the time must come when it will control the future and distance unravel to the end of time—this small round package of power, this force for lingering life or lingering death, this salt for the soul, this spice with roots in antiquity—this coated equation smaller than a fingertip embodies and contains you. And who gave it that right, who harnessed chemistry and put *things* in charge? We demand to know. We intend to hold them responsible: death would be too good for them. The search begins in the home, it begins just behind the mirror: there, in the bathroom cabinet, are the innocuous masters of our lives—the toothpaste, the deodorant, the shampoo. Someone has decreed that we should not remain during the days those briny, glistening starfish as which we crawled the bottoms of seas to suck up the smallest, reddest forms of life. It is not so bad to be in the air now, routine to live as two beings: one in the light, the other just beneath the light-tight skin of sleep. But to be the third thing: the creature that was given, by mistake, the demented brain, and now must absorb with flaccidity the daily dose of electricity that will prolong its self-knowledge. For it is one thing to be alive—the grass is alive, the pea and the potato grow, and microscopic algae stain with their living bodies the snow of the coldest regions—and another thing to *know* that one is alive. Where in philosophy was it decided that, if it is good to be able to choose, it is twice good to realize it? The argument that once raged inside the spiral corridors of a nautilus, at a depth a human being could only imagine, sings all around us like wind in the alleys, like city water in the sewers. We have not been shocked enough yet. We are not yet ready. Great areas of our brains still lie dormant like the liquid-carved underside of a coral reef. The debate rages in words and gestures. Sparks open up new hallways between logic and instinct. But it is in the dormant regions of the brain, the resonant cavities of absolute not-knowing, that life is closest to the source of life. A whole brain like that is like a head carried in on a plate. For a moment, it is one thing that looks like another thing. For a moment, everyone in the room could have sworn that it could see them, and that it blinked.

Long Island

The things I did, I did because of trees,
wildflowers and weeds, because of ocean and sand,
because the dunes move about under houses built on stilts,
and the wet fish slip between your hands back into the sea,
because during the War we heard strafing across the Bay
and after the War we found shell casings with our feet.
Because old tires ringed the boat docks,
and sandbags hung from the prows of speedboats,
and every road in every country ends at the water,
and because a child thinks each room in his house big,
and if the truth be admitted, his first art galleries
were the wallpaper in his bedroom and the carlights
warming the night air as he lay in bed counting.

The things I did, I counted in wattage and ohms,
in the twelve zones that go from pure black to pure white,
in the length of the trumpet and the curves of the cornet,
in the cup of the mouthpiece. In the compass and protractor,
in the perfect bevelled ruler, in abstract geometry,
and if the truth be known, in the bowing of cattails
he first read his Heraclitus and in the stretching box turtle
he found his theory of relativity and the gist of knowledge.
He did what he did. The action of his knee in walking
was not different from the over-stretching of an ocean wave,
and the proofs of triangles, cones and parallelograms
were neither more nor less than the beauty of a fast horse
which runs through the numbers of the stopwatch and past the finish.

The things I counted, I counted beyond the finish,
beyond rolling tar roadways that squared the fields,
where I spun on the ice, wavered in fog, sped up or idled,
and, like Perry, like Marco Polo, a young man I saw
alone walk unlit paths, encircled by rushes
and angry dogs, to the indentations of his island.
And if the truth be told, he learned of Columbus,
of Einstein, of Michelangelo, on such low roads and local waters.
Weakfish hauled weakening from the waters at night,
and the crab rowing into the light, told him in their way
that the earth moved around the sun in the same way,
with the branched mud-print of a duck's foot to read,
and life in the upturned bellies of the fishkill in the creek.

CLASSIFIED

I am no more stupid now than I ever was; I am the same.
The end of tomorrow is no further away than it ever was.
If no one had occasionally moved them, or fuelled them,
the end of our todays would be frozen like a field of old bolts
in their military silos, and wouldn't that be a kick
in the flowers for all the earthshaking dreams that caught us.
Wanted: a few good men and women who won't do their jobs.

She Can't Stop Herself

Where is "desire like a leaf without a twig?"
Where are "these things, our things?"
Where are the "angels bad or good?" All those things
that contain the poems of men and women. One begins
with nothing more than the angle of the sun
on a field of beans in spring—when things are right.
He has the feeling; he has the words. Another
says she saw the trees trying to move on,
with their fingers to their mouths to say hush.
She says it's the truth; she says she can't stop herself.
With eyes happy or sad, with blessings or curses,
with a racing pulse or a failing one,
with no time left or all the time in the world—
somehow men and women free themselves again and again
into speech—I said "free," but I misspoke.
For some it's just the dammed-up day,
the covered windows, the clouds, the shadows.
For others, it's the unexpected length of a summer afternoon.
You see: even such sentiment as this will do—
the wash, the beautiful sad colors of a wind that does not last,
desire that has its effect on us,
the things that are, for a while, our things,
the angels good or bad whom sometimes we astonish.

Song for a Little Bit of Breath

to Dorothy

I still have this vertical pain under my left shoulder blade.
Sometimes in the morning, the roadway by the front door
has this slick layer of new rain over it,
and the ground gets frost, and the grass its white hair.
I've got this finger tip of open space on my scalp
that once took stitches, and a slice through my right eyebrow
that took stitches, and a streak remains on my forehead
where recently we were together when the door hit me.

Some of our quietest moments lay either side of thunder.
Around us, lightning lit all—we were there to see it.
Our back porch stretched out into the middle of shooting stars,
and we felt a little bit of breath go out on each trail.
I still have this pain that falls through the entire night sky
in my shoulder, where, when the thunder has stopped,
your head has lain on my arm for twenty-five years.
I am taking bolts of lightning to cure it, and the space
around the thunder is a cure. But I wish on every star,
falling or not, that it isn't taken from me here.

Music Lessons

The best place to hear a cornet played is the local gymnasium:
the kind with a basketball court, a stage and a balcony
in which small public schools hold their songfests and dances.
The long waxy strips of the wooden floor are very like
the golden sounds of the B-flat cornet in bright daylight,
and the empty room in which so many bodies have passed
accepts and embraces each articulated musical phrase
with that warm sadness known best by the adolescent.

If I had never taken up the cornet, I sometimes think,
beauty would not have taken all my days and filled my thoughts.
If I had not had that free hour in the middle of the school day,
not selected a mouthpiece with a deep cup for its richer tone,
not carried it in my hand to warm it up ahead of time,
if I had never given in to the subtleties of an embouchure,
I would not have been blown about by every passing song,
each with its calendar and clock, each with its beloved.

It takes only a few measures for the dreams to get out,
and then you cannot stop them or make them go away.
A river of whole tones sweeps from the bell of the horn,
containing the sun and moon, the grass and the flowers,
all time, and the face of every kindness done to a boy,
and every object of his desire by name, and a single smile.
It was my good fortune to be the breath of a magic cornet
and my fate to fall asleep to music every night thereafter.

In My Nature: 3 Corrective Dialogues

To a Tree

Pine with little pines, with many arms,
with hair to sift the sunlight, with feet that grip
widely and deep, with a trunk for a spine—
you're my neighbor now, here at my window, bursting
to testify: *you can make it through the winter
in your heart. I did.* And it did, and does.

My heart was cold and hard like yours. Mine was
hidden in a fist, in a knot, like yours, mine
was mine alone. The world was snow, was covered—
if anything beat below the surface, I could not feel
it—me, the rock, the potato brought to term, me,
to whom all things were done while I stayed in this place.

I'm the kind who couldn't pick up the axe except
to lean it against the shed. I leaned it against the wind.
I shouldered it. Even after I let it fall,
I shouldered it. Today, with my blood running
and your sap running, and the world counting its shovels,
I wake to the rhythm of your Medusa load of axe handles.

The Tree Replies

To be a man is to be a sentimentalist, soft inside.
You don't stand but already you imagine a horizon
past the horizon, a purer arc of earth, a heaven—
and a pulsing under all: under snow, under soil.
Unhappy and remote, walking your eyes up a mountain
in steps, gauging the time available to you, alas,

yelling and straining, patronized by the stars,
radical, soft-living, harvested by any boss,
you swallow hard whenever you feel sleep approaching.
I'm going to give you another chance. Be like me.
Or, if it's late in your life, and you wish to be
remembered as noble, be like the axe in the air.

You can get a lot of comfort from standing up to
what doesn't move. And standing down, too—*there's*
the hard-won secret of dark places where the eyes
widen: at the bottom of the well, where the roots are,
among feelers inching toward the last drops of water.
Be willing to live like me. Be willing to die.

To the Rain

The rain fell down the length of the Eiffel Tower.
The rain fell the length of every tree on the lawn,
it crossed the desert of every window pane,
it gave the sun the appearance of a second thought,
it cut the smell of sulphur and the smell of sap,
we were open-gilled and it went right through us.

The clean rain is like the peeling spine, papery,
of an important book title—it comes to mean the day
as words come to mean the things they wrap around,
as I come to mean my love all night in my arms.
The clean rain is a push against the wool blankets,
the unfolding of wings in the City of Lights.

And I would ask it if it knows just why it is loved
and where the luck lives in scrap iron, landfill lives,
that the fish should writhe in lethal rapture
to stuff itself with things so small it takes a lifetime,
while this clean rain dents the land, and the sea
shudders from the sharp movements of convulsive breeders.

The Rain Replies

To be a man is to live a topside life, thrust out,
to be forced to breathe air, to swallow and to know
that life no longer passes through you intravenously.
My voice reminds you of the blue inside of the cloud
in which you grew, of a time with closed eyes,
of the nine months you lay in limpidity, creating an island.

If now you ask of the rain, born everywhere at once,
just why it is loved, replies arrive palms-up in the pines,
in columnar mountain springs and slid rivers—just past,
and in the negative of those desert plants which split
red flowers screaming forth in my absence.
I act because I am helpless not to. It brings me love.

Thus, in ten hundred, in Hangchow, Su Tungpo came
to the life on West Lake, with monks and sing-song women.
Bear with me, endure me. The boatmen were of two kinds:
those who fed the people, and those who sold their fish
to be thrown back—for such was a way to lay up heavenly treasure.
If caught, the same fish might save three lives from Hell.

To an Island

The world isn't pine trees and rain, all pebbles
just small enough to carry the obliquities of the poet
and the odd ironies of the French paragraph-poem.
The rain falls on the food of pigs and dogs,
the evergreen gets its life squeezed out by a set fire,
and the pebble—the pebble is a hand grenade writ small.

They always take away the land where it looks over water.
They have priced it so highly I can barely afford
to live near a tree. The ocean is a receding rumor.
Island known as Long Island, I call on you now
to rise against the rich, to arch your peninsular back
and throw off the cod-like purveyors of private beaches.

Am I angry with nature? No, I love you as I love
my own nature, your body as I love my own. Listen,
you can hear in me the wind that caressed my island
and see in me the shifting dunes and shell-laden tideline.
It is as if a drum were beaten in the streets
far from my island, and I heard an ocean hammering a shore.

The Island Replies

To be a man is to be said no to, principally
by others but occasionally, as now, by oneself.
I am giving you this chance: to leave the Island forever
which in any case is lost to you as a tree is lost
in an unexplored wood. It was your father's island:
his choice, his destination, his finny life-expiring life.

You are a man obsessed with the top twenty-five feet
of the sea, wherein the fish swell like bright flags—
fabulous oranges, reds, lavender—and crustaceans appear
to breathe, exhaling an oxidizing powder that bloodies the bottom.
And yet the blueing agency of deep water is most of it below,
as the wind and sand you contain is little more than your skin.

Also, those who scribble about me are little more than sandcrabs.
They burrow lightly, and etch lightly, and weigh little.
They are to be honored before the sand sweeps them away.
Is this what you want—to retreat, to be scoured and buried
because you could not bear to leave even one love behind?
Get out of here. Salvage what you can. The rest is imperceptible.

Ten Thousand Questions Answered

1   *Watching an Orange Moon Rise over Port Townsend Bay*

It is close, large, moving up rapidly.
And it rises where Mount Rainier stood in the light.
For a moment it rests on the summit of an unseen mountain.
A pinprick of light in the sky passes behind it.
So-and-so, the poet, says four lines in a stanza are too few.

2   *To a Pipefish Washed Up on the Beach*

Lying in mud, you escaped the life of bait.
The destiny of the pipefish—shiny, slender, electric—
is to become an offering to a larger catch.
Therefore, you lived longer by dying slowly.

3

Nothing is sadder than a book of poetry.
Before the book is begun, no sadness.
After the first poem, before the final poem—
there is no sadness before a thing is finished.
But afterwards, one grieves for one's failure.
The answer is to let the poem be too long to finish.

Our Neighbor's Cake

1 *On a Hot Day*

Today I prefer the cup to the coffee,
and the woven straw coaster underneath to the cup,
and the cool dark space underneath the table,
and the smoke already rising from the coming winter!

2 *On a Portrait of Myself*

Too fat! The artist did not succeed.
Too short! The man who did this doesn't see.
Too haggard! Does he think all my days the same?
Too dumb! This painter truly has no future.

3 *To a Raccoon*

You shake the metal cans until the stones
which keep the covers on the garbage rock.
Then you jump back three paces to wait.
Here, no need to make it seem the house is falling.
We will give you our neighbor's cake to eat.

4 *Nothing Missing*

I left many towns over many years.
The gods did not come down to see me off.
They sent the animals to watch me go.
Above me the birds set the telephone line humming.
Dogs left their territories and cats turned their heads.
I felt the whole world leaving alongside.
Wherever I went to stay, there was nothing missing.

Six Poems to Tao Yuan-ming

1

A friend first showed me your poems.
No words had meant more to her as a young woman.
This morning, fifteen centuries after you left,
I pull the curtain to the side, and the sun enters,
just as you said it would.
How can I not believe today in the illusions of the world?

2

Old man, do you know the good luck I have had?
Is there a place where you sit drinking wine,
hearing the whistling of hermits and the shimmering of continents?
Once we know our lot we go on without further doubt, you said.
Sometimes I cannot tell if these are my tracks
or those of a small animal of remote ways.

3   *To a Friend Who Has Been to the Dentist*

Two teeth lighter! And more to come out!
Like an old, toothless lion,
soon you will have to munch butterflies with your gums.
Don't despair, my friend. You look better than ever.
There's more room in your mouth now for drink and song,
now that those old canine molars have gone to the boneyard.
Are we ever really happy with all we have?

4   *Politics*

In a remote portion of a thick forest,
the limb of a tree struck by lightning still smokes.
The baker goes to his shop in the pre-dawn.
And the mountains appear to us gradually out of a mist
like the tallest pieces in a potter's kiln,
burning behind the little hand-made kiln-god.

5   *Two Kites in a Park*

One, a series of fourteen smaller kites, evenly spaced.
The lightness of them together, a kite of many kites:
the pattern is that of formal beauty; our pleasure is great.
We could look at this beautiful object forever.
It is as regular and various as a masterful sonnet.

High above it, a lone bird-like kite of red paper.
Moving without pattern, it seems to be trying to escape.
It struggles and relinquishes. It soars and falls and soars sharply.
It cuts unnameable shapes in air. We may say that it is "free,"
the more so as the string is invisible at such a height.
But we may never say of it that it is a sonnet.
Not to be able to say so gives us much to discuss among friends,
though none doubts that it is a kite.

6

We spend our days arguing over unimportant poems.
Sometimes we grow angry even before the first drink of wine.
Our skin is cracked like men who talk loudly.
The self-confident writer has mountainous aspirations.
We wish only to live until the end of this evening.

Considering My Words under the Wild Cherry Tree

Already twenty-two years have elapsed
since I went from student to teacher.
Since then, happy and unhappy,
each day I have talked to myself, seriously,
of the value of life, the nature of good,
my own shortcomings, the illusions of time,
the hatreds of men and women,
and other notions, abstract or otherwise.
I have often had to pick from my hair and collar
the leaves which fell there
while I was lost in thought, and my style of dress
is indeed a joke among successful writers.
No doubt regret is the price I pay
for these conversations, but do not pity me.
Everyone I ever loved, I still love.
The tricks I played with light as a boy
I can still perform. I am rarely cold.
It is true that my terrain is ignorance,
that often I lean against this tree in exhaustion,
that solace is as close as I may ever come to goodness.
Yet one must not underestimate the pleasures
of clear thought and clear words
when each must appear out of night and nothingness
as elsewhere rocks emerge from morning fog.
Already, twenty-two years have passed
since I went from student to teacher:
so long ago, it might have been yesterday.

After a Line by Theodore Roethke

In the vaporous grey of early morning,
on the mudflats of the moon, in grey feeling,
walking among boulders uncovered by minus-tides,
I am also still in the still hallway of dream,
facing a stairway without end, in a night without wires,
some recollection hanging in the air, whose image,
unapproachable in the night, waits out there.

Nothing to be gained but rain, and the burning of rain,
this day beginning with such thirst, such capacity
that everything may come to be again in reverse:
a world uncreated, a planet no one is watching—
not even we ourselves—now rising out of misty nothingness,
so that first stones are not solitary nor beings lonely,
nor water divided, nor continents discrete.

Joy to be wordless yet wide awake,
walking by water, in the midst of an unsubstantial suspense,
in clear sight of mist, in mud that sponges up the way back,
in the sight of the closed eyes of one still sleeping,
and there to be gathering shape and form
like a long whip of seaweed being inexorably washed ashore,
and now a head of hair stirring to bring love back which was gone.

MARVIN BELL is the author of eight books of poetry, a collection of essays and (with William Stafford) a volume of poems written as correspondence. Born August 3, 1937 in New York City, he grew up in Center Moriches, on the south shore of eastern Long Island. His honors include the Lamont Award of the Academy of American Poets for his first major collection, fellowships from the National Endowment for the Arts and the Guggenheim Foundation, and Senior Fulbright Appointments to Yugoslavia and Australia. He now divides his time between Iowa City, Iowa, where he is Flannery O'Connor Professor of Letters at The University of Iowa, and Port Townsend, Washington.